You Are Blessed

You Are Blessed

Taiwo Adesina

Published—2013

ISBN: 978-1-909787-08-7

Published by Purpose2Destiny TK Limited

All scripture quotations are taken from the New King James Version (NKJV) unless otherwise indicated.

Other scriptures used are The New International Version (NIV) and The Amplified Bible (AMP)

(Small letter "s" is used in satan and not capitalized so as not to glorify him)

Dedication

To My God and Father – I thank You for the bountiful blessings that you have bestowed upon me and which you are continuing to bestow upon me.
Being alive is a blessing.

Acknowledgement

I thank my brother, Pastor Adebowale Adesina for his encouragement, insight, input and guidance given to me during the completion of this book and Georgina Chong-You for editing this book. I further thank Jumoke Ademola of Gemsjummy Photography who took the photo for the back cover of this book.

Contents

Introduction

"However many blessings we expect from God, His infinite liberality will always exceed all our wishes and our thoughts."
-John Calvin

The Lord has promised to bless and multiply us and set His sanctuary in our midst. God is extremely generous and will always exceed all our wishes and our thoughts. God's blessings make us rich and do not add sorrow to our life. He has blessed us in the heavenly realms with every spiritual blessing in Christ Jesus and therefore lack and/or scarcity is not our portion and must not be permitted. God's blessing does not cease with life's setbacks; it is all encompassing. God has placed us on earth to be blessed and to be a blessing so that He can establish His covenant of peace with us.

Psalm 65:10 confirms that God's promises of blessing includes watering our fields, making our soil soft and soaking our seed with His rain, resulting in our crop yielding abundantly.

Equally, Ezekiel 34:2 states that God has promised to make us and the places round about our hill a blessing and He will cause the showers to come down on us in their due season. This shows us that there is no room for dryness, scarcity or lack in our lives. **Daniel W. Whittle, 1883** sang about God's promise to shower us with His blessing in the popular hymn—"There shall be showers of blessing". We need to appropriate this promise for ourselves.

The presence of the Holy Spirit in the life of the believer is also a sign of God's blessing as this is part of the blessings inherited by the believer. Jesus Christ prayed that His Spirit would remain in us and lead us at all times. He assures us that the Holy Spirit would reveal all things to us so that we would not walk in darkness.

You must not let fear, other peoples' opinion, or procrastination hinder you from taking hold of God's blessings. God says that you should step out in faith and take hold of what is rightfully yours as today is your day of salvation. God's blessings will distinguish you from others. There is certainly a marked difference between those who are blessed of the Lord and those who are not.

Having gone through life's challenges myself, such as having an identity crisis, being fearful and anxious and then overcoming these only makes me realise how far I have come. I now realise that being able to overcome these challenges is a blessing from God. I may not yet have all that I desire but God's past faithfulness gives me assurance that He will perfect all that concerns me.

God is in control of your life, He will not abandon you to fate; your plans and intents may be in your heart but it is God who sanctions them. God is never absent from your life and He will determine its outcome if you allow Him to.

God's blessings come with endless possibilities; there is nothing too difficult for Him to do. When God says that He has given us the ability to do great exploits, He means absolutely nothing is impossible for us to achieve in His Name. As you begin to read through this book, I pray that God will open your eyes and heart to receive all the Blessings He has in store for you.

Chapter 1

God Created You To Be Blessed and To Be a Blessing

When God created Man, He BLESSED Man. As you are God's creation, you too are blessed. You are blessed because of WHO YOU ARE IN GOD and not because of what YOU DO. You are BLESSED when you go to bed at night knowing that God watches over you, when you wake up in the morning to live another day, when you have food on your table and when you can pay your bills etc. Divine healing, good health, happiness, long life, joy, peace are all signs of God's blessings. Being physically, mentally, emotionally and financially sound are equally signs of His blessings. You are still BLESSED when you feel tired, weary and burned-out or when you have made a mistake.

As a Blessed child of God, He expects YOU TO BE A BLESSING TO OTHERS so that Glory can be brought to His Name. In order to appreciate what it means to be blessed and to be a blessing, let us look at the words "Blessed" and 'Blessing' as used in the Dictionary and Amplified Bible.

'Blessed' (Dictionary.reference.com):

Adjective

- Worthy of adoration, reverence, or worship: the Blessed Trinity.
- Consecrated; sacred; holy; sanctified: the Blessed Sacrament.
- Divinely or supremely favored; fortunate: to be blessed with a strong, healthy body; blessed with an ability to find friends
- Blissfully happy or contented.

'Blessing' (Oxford English Dictionary.com):

Noun

- The act or words of a person who blesses.
- A favour or gift bestowed by God, thereby bringing happiness.
- A special favour, mercy, or benefit: *the blessings of liberty.*

'Blessed' (The Amplified Bible—Psalm 1:1):

- happy, fortunate, prosperous and enviable

We can see that the words blessed and blessing includes being blissfully happy, contented, consecrated, sanctified, healthy, fortunate, prosperous, receiving a special favour/gift from God and being bestowed divine favour by God. Furthermore the definition of blessing includes granting a special favour, mercy, or benefit to others.

God intends us to be blessed in every area of our lives (*Ephesians 1:3*), as such it is our responsibility to grasp hold of His blessings in the realm of the spirit by faith and cause them to manifest in the realm of the physical. He also expects us to be a channel of blessing to others.

You Were Created To Be Blessed

Blessed—Old Testament:

Genesis 1: 28-30 records God's mandate to Man at creation. When God blessed Man, He commanded Man:

1. To be Fruitful

God's blessing of fruitfulness means that whatever you lay your hands on will result in fruitfulness and productivity. You won't be able to hide the results of your blessings as they will overflow and overspill for all to see. God's blessings will make you profitable in all your endeavours. You will produce good, tangible and exceptional results (the seeds you produce will yield much fruit). You have been created to be fertile and you are earmarked for success. You will surely become useful, purposeful and effective. Streams of water will flow through you to your surroundings.

2. To Multiply

You have been commissioned to multiply and increase to such an extent that the world will have no choice but to take notice of you. You have been commissioned to produce a hundred fold return in whatever you sow (Mark 10:30). Not only will you multiply on your own account, all those around you will also reap from your Godly fortune. You will produce protégés to become achievers like yourself. God wants us to multiply in every area of our lives. He also expects the Church to increase and move forward. He wants the leaders, pastors and workers to continue in their service of Him so that more souls can be won for His Kingdom.

3. To Fill the Earth

God expects you to fill the earth with all that He has bestowed on you. He has filled you up so that you can in turn pour out everything deposited inside of you. He expects you to impart your world, become a blessing to your family and to your generation. He has empowered you to complete your assignment on earth. You have been made complete from the time of your conception and therefore no matter how much you give, you will always be full. **God's blessings in your life cannot run dry.**

4. To Subdue the Earth by making use of all its vast resources in the service of God and Man

God owns the entire universe and all that is in it (*Psalms 24:1*); He owns all the resources on earth, which He has made available to us. He expects us to make use of everything that grows on the ground for our nourishment and benefit, He expects us to subdue the earth by taking charge of its resources and using them for His and man's benefit.

5. To Have Complete Dominion

God gave Man power, authority, control and dominion over every living creature including satan (*Psalms 8*). You must not give up this dominance and legal authority. God has mandated that you claim your territorial authority with confidence. He wants you to manage and care for what He has bequeathed to you.

After God had given His mandate to Adam and Eve they allowed the devil to deceive them into forfeiting it. They ate the fruit from the tree of the knowledge of good and evil resulting in them becoming naked and ashamed before the Lord. God sent them out of the garden in order to prevent them eating from the tree of life which would have allowed them to live perpetually on earth. He placed a cherub with a flaming sword to keep and guard the tree of life to prevent them eating from it.

However, despite man's fall, God restored man back to his original position in Himself through Jesus Christ, who has given us complete victory, authority and dominion over all things. In the book of John 1:12 we are told that as many as received Him (Jesus Christ) to them He gave the power to become children of God. It means that if we are God's children then, we and the Father are one; we can therefore do all things through Christ who strengthens us.

New birth in Christ ties us to a supernatural source in God, as God is the source of our inheritance.

In Deuteronomy 15:6, God promises us that when we walk in the financial authority He has given us we will lend to many nations but that we shall borrow from none (financial freedom); and that we shall rule over many nations and none shall rule over us (dominion and ruler-ship). This will only be possible if we become diligent and alert to taking possession of all that God has in store for us. God's financial blessings in your life will cause you to multiply and increase resulting in you being the head and never the tail.

God has given us the power to create wealth (*Deut 8:18*); He expects us to walk in faith to receive His wealth because when we do so, He will grant us our requests (*Matthew 7:7*). He also expects us to prosper in every area of our lives — financially, socially, mentally— and not just in our souls. We must endeavour to appropriate all that God has in store for us through Jesus Christ. God knows the plans that He has for us, which is to give us a future, hope and an expected end. He will provide you with what no eye has seen nor ear has heard of because He will overwhelm you with His blessings (1 *Corinthians 2: 9).*

You must seek God's kingdom first and His ways of doing things and everything else will follow (Matthew *6:33).*

In Deuteronomy 28: 2-13 (NIV) God outlines the blessings that will accompany you if you keep His commandments and walk in His ways. Obedience is required to take hold of these blessings, as God will not have it any other way:

- God will set you high above all the nations on earth.
- You will be blessed in the city and blessed in the country.
- The fruit of your womb will be blessed, and the crops of your land and the young of your livestock—the calves of your herds and the lambs of your flocks.
- Your basket and your kneading trough will be blessed.
- You will be blessed when you come in and blessed when you go out.
- The LORD will grant that the enemies who rise up against you will be defeated before you. They will come at you from one direction but flee from you in seven.
- The LORD will send a blessing on your barns and on everything you put your hand to. The LORD your God will bless you in the land He is giving you.
- The LORD will establish you as His holy people, as He promised you on oath,
- All the peoples on earth will see that you are called by the Name of the LORD, and they will fear you.
- The LORD will grant you abundant prosperity—in the fruit of your womb, the young of your livestock and the crops of your ground—in the land He swore to your forefathers to give you.
- The LORD will open the heavens, the storehouse of His bounty, to send rain on your land in season and to bless all the work of your hands. You will lend to many nations but will borrow from none.

- The LORD will make you the head, not the tail. You will always be at the top, never at the bottom.

To receive God's blessings you must have God as the centre and circumference of your life. Your primary motivation in life must be God; you must seek Him with all of your heart, soul and body. Your primary desire should be to please Him (*Psalms 37: 4*). When you do this, God promises to bless you and to bless the works of your hands; He promises to prosper whatever you lay your hands upon and bless wherever you go.

God states that His thoughts and ways are different from ours. Our idea of success is different from what God's idea of success is, therefore we should ask Him to reveal His ways and plans to us. Some think that their main purpose in life is to live for self, success, wealth, pleasure and/or fame but Apostle Paul states that life for him is the Lord Jesus Christ (*Philippians 1:21).* I pray that this too will be your primary motivation and reason for living. We must store up for ourselves treasures in heaven, which do not rust, cannot be destroyed or stolen because where our treasure is our heart will also be (*Matthew 6:20-21*).

For those who think that money and wealth is everything, 1 Timothy 6:7 and Psalms 49:17 states that you brought nothing into this world and you will take nothing out of it. If you decide to get buried with all your money, gold and best attire like the Egyptian Pharaohs did before you, you will be shocked, as we all know that their earthly possessions remained on earth in the tomb waiting to be excavated by Archaeologists or stolen by tomb raiders.

Our idea of success is different from what God's idea of success is.

1 Timothy 6:10-11 states that the love of money is a root of all evil and we should not allow ourselves to be led astray or wander from the faith by our craving for it. When you make money your obsession you will never get enough of it and you will continue to live in fear of losing it all.

Those who live for pleasure soon realise that a feeling of emptiness follows; examples of these can be seen in the lives of drug addicts and alcoholics who after having their fix, feel empty and require a higher dosage to experience that feeling of euphoria again. Likewise those who live for themselves often turn out to be greedy, selfish and self-centred and they end up being miserable, lonely and secluded because people do not want to be around them.

> *'For what will it profit a man if he gains the whole world, and loses his own soul? Or what will a man give in exchange for his soul?' (Mark 8:36-37).*

You will find that you have not gained anything but emptiness after amassing all the wealth in the world but do not have **Christ** or **love** for others.

> *'For all that is in the world—the lust of the flesh, the lust of the eyes, and the pride of life—is not of the Father but is of the world. And the world is passing away, and the lust of it; but he who does the will of God abides forever' (1 John 2: 16-17).*

Has God given you a dream that seems scary, unimaginable or unbelievable? I want you to know that He has placed all the resources on this earth needed to fulfil it at your disposal, as such He expects you to rise up to achieve your dreams. Are you dreaming of flying a plane, writing a book, setting up a business or going to the university; fulfil your dream by taking a day and step at a time as this will lead you to victory.

You may be middle aged or a senior citizen and wonder whether God can still bless you. I want you to know that God will, irrespective of your age bless you so that you can achieve the tasks He has given to you. Your only duty is to be faithful, obedient and dedicated to Him. In Joshua 14:6-15, Caleb came to Joshua when he was 85 years old at Gilgal and asked for his blessing (Land), which Moses had promised him when they were in the wilderness. Caleb asked Joshua for the Hill Country (Hebron) because he knew that he was still as strong to go out to battle as he was when he went out to spy the land of Canaan forty years earlier. As a result of his bold request Joshua gave him Hebron as his inheritance.

"Blessed"—New Testament

In Matthew 5:2-12 (NIV), Jesus taught the crowd who had come to listen to Him on what it meant to be blessed. He told them that whilst the Pharisees and Sadducees may not consider them blessed because of their social standing, God considered them blessed because of their relationship with Him. He taught the people that:

- Blessed are the poor in spirit, for theirs is the kingdom of heaven.
- Blessed are those who mourn, for they will be comforted.
- Blessed are the meek, for they will inherit the earth.
- Blessed are those who hunger and thirst for righteousness, for they will be filled.
- Blessed are the merciful, for they will be shown mercy.
- Blessed are the pure in heart, for they will see God.
- Blessed are the peacemakers, for they will be called sons of God.
- Blessed are those who are persecuted because of righteousness, for theirs is the kingdom of heaven.
- Blessed are they when people insult, persecute and falsely say all kinds of evil against them because of Him for great was their reward in Heaven.

Jesus also said the following about being blessed:-

- **Matthew 11: 6**—Blessed is the man who does not fall away on account of Him.
- **Luke 11: 28**—Blessed are those who hear the word of God and obey it.
- **Luke 14:15**—Blessed is the man who will eat at the feast in the kingdom of God.
- **John 20: 29**—Blessed are those who have not seen and yet have believed in Him.

As followers of Christ these blessings are available to us and we must endeavour to appropriate them for ourselves.

The New Testament closes by saying in:

- **Romans 4: 7-8**—Blessed are they whose transgressions are forgiven, whose sins are covered. Blessed is the man whose sin the Lord will never count against him.
- **2 Corinthians 9:8 (Amp)**—And God is able to make all grace (every favour and earthly blessing) come to you in abundance, so that you may always and under all circumstances and whatever the need be self-sufficient [possessing enough to require no aid or support and furnished in abundance for every good work and charitable donation].
- **James 1:12**—Blessed is the man who perseveres under trial, because when he has stood the test, he will receive the crown of life that God has promised to those who love him.
- **Revelation 20:6**—Blessed and holy are those who have a part in the first resurrection. The second death has no

power over them, but they will be priests of God and of Christ and will reign with him for a thousand years.
- **Revelation 22:14**—Blessed are those who wash their robes, that they may have the right to the tree of life and may go through the gates into the city.

You Were Created To Be A Blessing

God has blessed us so that we can be a blessing to our family, friends and community just like Abraham was.

'I will make you a great nation; I will bless you and make your name great; And you shall be a blessing' (Gen 12: 2).

God has blessed us so that He can establish His covenant of peace and prosperity with us (*Deut 8:18*), He does not expect us to hoard what He has given to us, rather He expects us to dispense goodness to others by touching the lives of those we come into contact with, as hoarding only leads to poverty and lack.

There is one who scatters, yet increases more; And there is one who withholds more than is right, But it leads to poverty. The generous soul will be made rich, and he who waters will also be watered himself. The people will curse him who withholds grain; But blessing will be on the head of him who sells it ' (Proverbs 11: 24-26).

You may ask yourself whom do I bless? The answer is simple. All you need to do is be obedient to God when He leads you to bless somebody as He will surely order your path and footsteps to the person He wants you to bless. God will instruct you on how to be a blessing to each person He leads you to, as such you need to be sensitive to His Spirit at all times so that you do not miss the opportunity of dispensing goodness.

I remember vividly an incident some years ago, when God prompted me to bless a relative who was facing financial challenges that I was not aware of. We had attended a church programme and throughout the service I felt God asking me to give her some money for her fare home. I felt embarrassed to ask her if she needed financial assistance as I believed that she was financially well off than I was. At the end of the programme, God notched me to ask her again, but I was beginning to feel uncomfortable of the thought that God will make such suggestions to me. As we boarded the bus home, she turned towards me and asked me quietly whether I could pay for her fare as she had no money. I discovered that day that she had lost her job and had been struggling to meet her basic needs. She said she had attended the programme because God had assured her that He will take care of her fare. I never forgot this experience.

You may be saying to yourself but 'I don't have much money',' I don't have a good job', 'I don't have the skills or abilities required', 'I can't cook or bake'. I want you to know that God will not ask you to give what you don't have as He will only ask you to account for what He has given you.

You can bless people in any of the following ways, the following list is however not exhaustive:

1) By giving unconditional love
2) By giving a listening ear
3) By giving your time
4) By taking someone out to lunch/dinner and picking up the tab/bill
5) By babysitting for a friend/family or church member
6) By baking a cake for others
7) By cooking for an elderly or sick relative/friend
8) By giving free tuition lessons to a child who needs extra help in maths, English, etc.

9) By helping someone pay their household bill/ paying for the grocery
10) By praying for others
11) By giving your money
12) By giving assistance /help to others

When you take care of others, God will take care of you as Proverbs 11:24-26 states that it is one who withholds from others who becomes poor whilst the one who is generous to others becomes rich. I pray that you will allow yourself to be used by God to bless others so that your own needs can be met.

Align yourself to God, and you will receive His blessings.

When you do God's Will and walk in His Way God will abide with you forever. In 1 Corinthians 10:24, we are told not to seek only our own welfare, good and advantage but rather we should seek the welfare and good of our neighbours. The result of which will cause God's Grace to abound mightily upon us.

'And God is able to make all grace (every favour and earthly blessing) come to you in abundance, so that you may always and under all circumstances and whatever the need be self-sufficient [possessing enough to require no aid or support and furnished in abundance for every good work and charitable donation]' 2 Corinthians 9:8 (AMP).

Jesus Christ came to the world to be a blessing to us. He came to this world to die for mankind so that through His death on the cross and subsequent Resurrection we may have life. He gave Himself for our sins and became a channel of blessing through which God bestowed salvation on all mankind. Since Jesus could sacrifice Himself for us, we too should be able to take the time out to be a blessing to others.

How then can you receive God's blessings?

A number of actions you can take to receive God's blessings include:

a) Meditating On God's Word-

When you meditate on God's word on a daily basis you will receive instructions from God regarding His promises for your life. By heeding and keeping watch on God's word you will find inner strength to wait for the manifestation of your blessings.

b) Spending Time in God's Presence-

In order to receive all that God has in store for you, you must take time out from the crowd. God wants to tell and show you many things He has planned for you. However, He will only tell and show them to you when you separate yourself from the multitude.

Prophet Habakkuk and Apostle John had to separate themselves from the crowd before they were able to hear and see what God had in store for them. Without their effort to move closer to God, their lives would have remained the same — mundane and boring.

'I will stand my watch and set myself on the rampart; And watch to see what He will say to me, And what I will answer when I am corrected. Then the LORD answered me and said: ' Write the vision . . . '(Habakkuk 2:1-2).

c) Trusting the Lord-

You must place your trust in the Lord and not in your own abilities, gifting or calling. You must not try to sort things out by yourself or in your own way, but allow God to bring to pass what He has promised. You must trust Him to deliver to you what He has promised.

'Lean on, trust in, and be confident in the Lord with all your heart and mind and do not rely on your own insight or understanding. In all your ways know, recognize, and acknowledge Him, and He will direct and make straight and plain your paths. Be not wise in your own eyes; reverently fear and worship the Lord. ..' Proverbs 3:5-7(AMP).

d) Humbling Yourself before the Lord-

You must submit yourself before the Lord and not allow pride, success or your gifting to get in your way as God states that He will exalt (promote) you in due season.

'Therefore humble yourselves [demote, lower yourselves in your own estimation] under the mighty hand of God, that in due time He may exalt you' 1 Peter 5:6 (AMP).

However, if you choose to allow pride and arrogance to lead you rather than His spirit, God states that He will set Himself up against you. I pray that God's spirit will be your guiding force at all times (*James 4:6).*

e) Walking in Faith-

As faith comes by hearing the word of God, you must soak yourself in His word so that when you pray and ask God for anything your prayers will be answered (*Romans 10:17*). When you pray do not waver or allow doubt in your mind as doing this prevents your prayers being answered (*James 1:6-7*).

Do not allow difficult situations, challenges or people steal your faith. When God gives you a word or promise, which requires you to take some corresponding action, step out in faith despite the challenging situations or unbelief of people around you and take hold of what God has promised; for we walk by faith in Christ and not by sight (*II Corinthians 5:7*).

> *'So also faith, if it does not have works (deeds and actions of obedience to back it up), by itself is destitute of power (inoperative, dead)' (James 2: 17 AMP).*

f) Fleeing from sin and living a Godly life-

> *'But the fruit of the [Holy] Spirit [the work which His presence within accomplishes] is love, joy (gladness), peace, patience (an even temper, forbearance), kindness, goodness (benevolence), faithfulness, Gentleness (meekness, humility), self-control (self-restraint, continence). Against such things there is no law that can bring a charge].'*
> *Galatians 5:22-23 (NKJV).*

In order for you to receive all that God has in store for you. You must not allow sin into your life because the devil would want to take advantage and gain a stronghold. You must place yourself in God's hands and under His control so that when the devil comes to tempt you, you can resist him in the name of the Lord and he would flee from you (*James 4:7*). You must not give into the cravings of the flesh but rather you should ask the Holy Spirit to help you in your times of weaknesses.

> *'I therefore, the prisoner for the Lord, appeal to and beg you to walk (lead a life) worthy of the [divine] calling to which you have been* ***called, with behaviour that is a credit to the summons to God's service****, Living as becomes you] with complete lowliness of mind (humility) and meekness (unselfishness, gentleness, mildness), with patience, bearing with one another and making allowances because you love one another. Be eager and strive earnestly to guard and keep the harmony and oneness of [and produced by] the Spirit*

in the binding power of peace'
Ephesians 4: 1-3 (AMP).

g) Renewing and Transforming Your Mind—

The 'Mind' is a battlefield. A spiritual battle occurs in the mind with the devil who wants to use his tricks to corrupt the mind and debar us from taking hold of our miracles and blessings (life partner, children, healing, financial and spiritual breakthrough). In order to successfully wage war against the devil we must put on the whole armour of God and use the weapons God has provided to us. **Paul lists the whole armour of God which are the weapons of our warfare in Ephesians 6:13-17 as truth, righteousness, the gospel of peace, faith, salvation and the Word of God**; these weapons are to be used to defeat satan in our minds.

God wants your thoughts to be in accordance with His Word because you can only get your heart's desires when you believe what His Word says concerning your life. You must believe that whatever you ask God for in prayer you shall receive as nothing is impossible for those that believe (Matthew 17.20). You must pull down every stronghold (a firm wrong conviction such as a habit, addiction or process that has become fixed), cast down imaginations (vain/false imaginations) and cast down every high thing that seeks to exalt itself against the knowledge and purpose of God in your life. You must bring into captivity every thought so that it is obedient to Christ, be willing to submit yourself to Christ and obey Him (2 Corinth 10:5-6), because when you do so, you will take hold of your blessings.

When you believe that you are not worthy of a blessing or you don't understand the value of a particular blessing you allow others to steal them from you without putting up a fight because you think you don't' deserve the blessing in the first place. I remember some years back when I bought myself a car from a car dealer, he gave me a brand new portable Global Positioning System (GPS) for free which I didn't know the value of. I had kept the GPS system in my garage for a year when my older brother asked me to give it to him if I didn't want it as it was a very important piece of equipment. I asked him what the GPS was and he gave me a lecture on its value. He helped me set it up so that I could use it when going to places I didn't know the directions to. I have since learnt the importance of this piece of equipment as I am now able to travel far and wide and go to places I would not have ventured to because of fear of losing my way. When I look back, I now realise that I could have lost this blessing because I was ignorant of its value. I pray that you would not lose what belongs to you to another due to ignorance in Jesus name.

Ask God to remove the negative feelings and thoughts you have about yourself so that you can receive His blessings. Once you renew your mind and no longer conform to the patterns of this world (for example the world says that Heaven only helps those who help themselves); you will become transformed from the inside out and nothing shall be capable of preventing you from taking hold of your blessing/miracles.

Do not conform any longer to the pattern of this world, but be transformed by the renewing of your mind. Then you will be able to test and approve what God's will is—his good, pleasing and perfect will Romans 12:2 (NIV).

h) Ridding yourself of the Older Brother Spirit—Luke 15: 11-32

The "Older Brother Spirit" can prevent us from receiving the blessings God has in store for us. God only promotes us when He knows our time for promotion is right as He looks at our spiritual growth and not our age or the amount of time we have spent in ministry. Self promotion is a disease that has found its way from the secular world into the church of Christ. It manifests itself through jealousy, envy, bitterness, covetousness and a failure to see the wider picture. Because of ingratitude a person neglects, ignores or devalues the blessings God has given him or her.

Church folks with this "older brother spirit" feel overlooked for promotion. They are concerned with "self". They feel that they have been overlooked by the Pastor or church committee and that they have not been accorded the same respect as their fellow brethren who have not spent the same number of years serving God diligently as they have done! They fail to realise that they are not spiritually mature to handle the responsibility that goes with the position. Don't get me wrong, there is nothing wrong with expecting to be appreciated or valued by others in the church but when we try to exalt ourselves for our own benefit or advantage to the detriment of our fellow believers we need to take a good look at ourselves.

Self righteousness or pride can also prevent believers from taking hold of the blessings God has in store for them. They become self absorbed in their own desires or wants and they feel spiritually superior to those struggling with issues in their lives—unknown to them this is just a spirit of religiosity.

The best way to overcome the older brother spirit is to ask God to show you how much He values you and to make you understand that you are already part of the "Body of Christ" and without you the Church will not function as it ought to. When you begin to have a heart of gratitude and joy, you will begin to enjoy fellowship with other believers.

You are more than what people see. You are the embodiment of Christ and you have been filled up with every spiritual blessing (Ephesians 1:3-14). Ask God to make you content in all circumstances and to have the boldness to take hold of your blessings without fear or unworthiness. You are deserving and worthy to ask God to bless you with all good things.

i) Praising God—

When you praise God for who He is, you remove the focus from yourself and on to Him. When you praise God He will inhabit your praise *(Psalms 22:3)*. He will tabernacle with you resulting in Him fulfilling His promises to bless you and your family. When you praise God He will intervene on your behalf because your praise delights, glorifies and edifies Him.

> *'Though the fig tree may not blossom, Nor fruit be on the vines; Though the labour of the olive may fail, And the fields yield no food; Though the flock may be cut off from the fold, And there be no herd in the stalls— Yet I will rejoice in the LORD, I will joy in the God of my salvation. The LORD God is my strength; He will make my feet like deer's feet, And He will make me walk on my high hills' Habakkuk 3: 17-19 (NKJV).*

j) Obeying God –

As previously outlined obedience is required to take hold of God's blessings, as God will not have it any other way.

God's greatest desire is to see you walk in the authority, dominion and power, which He bestowed upon you at creation. It is His desire to see you blessed and to be a blessing to your generation. I pray that you will rise up with boldness and take hold of all that God has destined for you and that you will be a blessing to your generation.

Chapter 2

The Holy Spirit in the Life of the Believer

The Holy Spirit is the Spirit of God. He is the third person of the Trinity (Father, Son and Holy Spirit). As part of the Godhead, the Holy Spirit is equal with God the Father and with God the Son. The Holy Spirit is a real Person who came to live within followers of Jesus Christ after Jesus rose from the dead and ascended to heaven. The presence of the Holy Spirit in the life of the believer is a sign of God's blessing. The Holy Spirit helps us retain the numerous blessings God has bestowed upon us. God gifts His Spirit to believers at salvation when they accept Jesus Christ as their personal Lord and Saviour.

Jesus prayed for His disciples and for future believers just before his departure that His Spirit would lead us at all times. He promised us that when the Holy Spirit comes that He would guide us in all truth thereby preventing us from falling into error; that He would not speak His own message but the message (Word) that the Father had given Him concerning us.

Jesus Christ assured us that the Holy Spirit would reveal to us what would happen in the future so that we will not walk in darkness; that He will bring glory to Him (Jesus Christ) because He will take from what is His (Jesus) and reveal His (Jesus Christ) message to us.

> *'But when he, the Spirit of truth, comes, he will guide you into all truth. He will not speak on his own; he will speak only what he hears, and he will tell you what is yet to come. He will bring glory to me by taking from what is mine and making it known to you. All that belongs to the Father is mine. That is why I said the Spirit will take from what is mine and make it known to you ' John: 16:13-15(NIV).*

The above scripture shows that the Holy Spirit is working with the Father and Son in unity to bestow God's heavenly and divine blessings upon us. Jesus Christ referred to the Holy Spirit as a Person (He) and not a thing (It), power or energy. Jesus Christ said that the Holy Spirit would reveal what He has heard from Him (Jesus) and not pursue His own agenda; this clearly shows again that the Father, Son and Holy Spirit are working as one to promote you. Jesus Christ explained the exact role of the Holy Spirit to avoid any misunderstanding that may arise. **He said that the Holy Spirit's role is to Comfort, Help, Strengthen and Advocate on the believers' behalf before the Father (God) John 14:16**. The Holy Sprit has not come to bring condemnation to the believer but rather He has come to help us in our times of weaknesses and to convict us of sin so that we can acknowledge our guilt and repent.

After Jesus' death and resurrection, He revealed Himself to His disciples and reiterated His promises of sending His Holy Spirit; He told His disciples that when the Holy Spirit came upon them they would receive power and they would become His witnesses in Jerusalem, Judea, and Samaria and to the ends of the earth, (*Acts 1:3-8*). On the day of Pentecost, the Holy Spirit descended upon the disciples and those who were praying in the room, and they all began to speak in different foreign languages according to the ordinance given to them by the Holy Spirit.

The role and function of the Holy Spirit cannot be ignored in our lives as believers. We need God's Spirit for the following reasons:

1) To help us succeed in life, as we can't do anything in our own strength — Zechariah: 4:6.
2) To help us overcome evil and the works of the devil — Matthew 12:28.
3) To give us faith –John 3: 1-15.
4) To reveal all truth in the scriptures to us about Jesus Christ –John 5:39; John 16:13.
5) To Comfort, Counsel, Help, Advocate and Strengthen us – John 14: 16.
6) To empower us for the tasks that God has given us — Acts 1: 8.
7) To Counsel and help us make the right decisions in life— Acts 13:2; Acts 16:6.
8) To help us put to death the deeds of the flesh –Romans 8:12-13.
9) To help us pray –Romans 8:26.
10) To build us up — Romans 8: 27.
11) To justify and Sanctify us — 1 Corinthians 6:11.
12) To give us His Wisdom, knowledge and understanding.
13) To give us His gifts, achievements and abilities — 1 Corinthians 12
14) To seal us to Jesus Christ — II Corinthians 1:22, Ephesians 1:13.
15) To free us from bondage — II Corinthians 3:17.
16) To give us liberty; where the spirit of the Lord is there is liberty —
II Corinthians 3:17.

17) To Produce in us the fruits of His Spirit — Galatians 5: 22-23.
18) To let us know of our Sonship with God (that we are the children of God) — 1 John 3:1.
19) To lead and draw us to Christ so that we can receive salvation — Revelation 22:17.
20) To help us in our service in Christ.

You can receive the gift of the Holy Spirit through any of the following ways:

1) **Salvation** — By accepting Jesus Christ as your personal Lord and Saviour. Jesus Christ promises to fill you with His spirit and cause His spirit to flow continuously in and through you *(John 7: 37-39).*
2) **Repenting of your sins** – when you repent of your sins and ask God to baptise you with His Spirit He will do so.

'Peter replied, "Repent and be baptized, every one of you, in the name of Jesus Christ for the forgiveness of your sins. And you will receive the gift of the Holy Spirit. The promise is for you and your children and for all who are far off—for all whom the Lord our God will call'
—Acts 2: 38-39(NIV).

The Holy Spirit will empower you to win souls for Christ just like Peter did. You will also overcome the works of the devil as God states that you cannot overcome satan in your own strength but by His Spirit alone.

3) **Praying in faith** — Jesus Christ states that you should pray for the power of the Holy Spirit and that you must not cease in your prayers. He wants you to pray in faith so that you will receive whatever you have asked for. When you ask God in faith to fill you with His Spirit, He will do so.

'Therefore I tell you, whatever you ask for in prayer, believe that you have received it, and it will be yours', Mark 11:24(NIV).

4) **Laying on of hands** –This happens when a pastor, priest or some other spirit—led/filled person lays their hands on you and asks God to release and fill you with His Spirit.

Then Peter and John placed their hands on them, and they received the Holy Spirit. When Simon saw that the Spirit was given at the laying on of the apostles' hands, he offered them money and said, "Give me also this ability so that everyone on whom I lay my hands may receive the Holy Spirit." Acts 8:17-19 (NIV).

Then Ananias went to the house and entered it. Placing his hands on Saul, he said, "Brother Saul, the Lord—Jesus, who appeared to you on the road as you were coming here—has sent me so that you may see again and be filled with the Holy Spirit" Act 9:17 (NIV).

When you imbibe the Holy Spirit, He will remain with you forever and will lead you on the right path, in the right direction and at the right time. All you need to do is be obedient to His leadings and promptings at all times. After receiving the Holy Spirit you must refrain from allowing the deeds of the flesh such as bitterness, rage, bad temper, malice, quarrelling, gossiping or evil speaking operate in your life as these things grieves the Holy Sprit and may cause Him to withdraw from you (*Ephesians 4:30-31*). You should allow the fruits of the Holy Sprit such as kindness to others; tender heartedness, forgiveness and loving kindness, guide and emanate from you (*Ephesians 4: 32; 5: 9*).

Manifestations of the Holy Spirit

Now there are distinctive varieties and distributions of endowments (gifts, extraordinary powers distinguishing certain Christians, due to the power of divine grace operating in their souls by the Holy Spirit) and they vary, but the [Holy] Spirit remains the same. And there are distinctive varieties of service and ministration, but it is the same Lord [Who is served]. And there are distinctive varieties of operation [of working to accomplish things], but it is the same God Who inspires and energizes them all in all. But to each one is given the manifestation of the [Holy] Spirit [the evidence, the spiritual illumination of the Spirit] for good and profit. To one is given in and through the [Holy] Spirit [the power to speak] a message of wisdom, and to another [the power to express] a word of knowledge and understanding according to the same [Holy] Spirit; To another wonder-working] faith by the same [Holy] Spirit, to another the extraordinary powers of healing by the one Spirit; To another the working of miracles, to another prophetic insight the gift of interpreting the divine will and purpose); to another the ability to discern and distinguish between [the utterances of true] spirits [and false ones], to another various kinds of [unknown] tongues, to another the ability to interpret [such] tongues. All these [gifts, achievements, abilities] are inspired and brought to pass by one and the same [Holy] Spirit, Who apportions to each person individually [exactly] as He chooses 1 Corinthians 12: 4-11(Amp).

The are nine (9) Manifestations of the Holy Spirit that can be gleamed from the above passage:

1) Word of wisdom through the Spirit
2) Word of knowledge through the same Spirit
3) Faith by the same Spirit
4) Gifts of healings by the same Spirit
5) The working of miracles
6) Prophecy
7) Discerning of spirits
8) Different kinds of tongues
9) Interpretation of tongues

The Holy Spirit distributes these workings to everyone He deems fit and there is no limit to the number each individual can receive. These workings however cannot operate in a vacuum, they must be utilized effectively for the body of Christ. When operating under these gifting or when others are ministering to us we need to be careful and test every spirit, as the devil and his demons can copy every manifestation and gift of God for their own gain and motive.

> *'Beloved, do not believe every spirit, but test the spirits, whether they are of God; because many false prophets have gone out into the world. By this you know the Spirit of God: Every spirit that confesses that Jesus Christ has come in the flesh is of God, and every spirit that does not confess that Jesus Christ has come in the flesh is not of God . . .' –(1 John 4:1—3).*

The Symbols of the Holy Spirit

There are a number of symbols that apply to the Holy Spirit. The Bible uses symbols to give us a better understanding of the Holy Spirit and of His workings. We must not fall into the trap of those who believe that symbols are the Holy Spirit Himself and then idolise or worship these symbols.

- **Dove**—At the end of the flood Noah released a dove that returned with a fresh olive branch in its beak to signify newness of life (*Genesis 8: 8-12*). At Jesus Christ's baptism the Holy Spirit came down upon Him and remained with Him in the symbol of a dove. John saw a dove descend out of heaven and rested on Jesus never to depart *(John 1:32).*

- **Cloud and Light**—God covered Moses with His cloud on Mount Sinai in the wilderness. God also covered Israel with His cloud by day to keep them cool and His fire by night to keep them warm. Furthermore, during the ascension of

Jesus Christ the cloud took Jesus out of the sight of His disciples *(Acts 1: 6-11).*

- **Fire**—Fire warms, purifies and refines—we see this symbol's operation in the life of Elijah who called down fire from heaven to burn the sacrifice he was offering to God on Mount Carmel to signify God's presence. On the Day of Pentecost the Holy Spirit came upon the disciples in the form of cloves of fire. The Bible often reiterates that we should not quench the Spirit, referring to the Spirit's symbol of fire *(1 Thessalonians 5:19-22).*

- **Oil**—Oil is used to lubricate and eliminate friction. This symbol can be seen in the life of Aaron and the Priests who were consecrated and anointed with oil, which was poured on their heads to anoint them for service. Oil was used to keep lamps burning in the Holy Place and to anoint the sick. We have also been given the mandate to anoint the sick amongst us with oil (James 5:14). In Psalm 92:10 the Psalmist said that he was anointed with fresh oil resulting in his cup overflowing. The anointing oil will make God's blessings flow towards you. In order to be effective in God's kingdom we need that continual anointing.

- **Living Water**—Water washes, refreshes and purifies. Jesus Christ referred to His Holy Spirit as His living water and stated that His Spirit would flow like living water in the believer *(John 7: 37-39).*

- **The Seal**—has been used to express God's mark of His Holy Spirit on believers. He seals believers to Himself for the day of redemption *(II Corinthians 1:22).*

- **The finger of God**—Moses received the tablets of stone written by the finger of God, which symbolised God's

Spirit. Jesus Christ stated that He used the finger of God to cast out demons signifying that it is by God's spirit alone that we can overcome the works of the devil. The finger of God further refers to the day of God's reckoning and judgement.

- **Wind**—The sound of the wind can be heard if you listen attentively *(John 3:8)*. Jesus referred to His Spirit as the wind when He said that the wind blows where it wills. This goes to show that we (believers) cannot box or restrict His spirit rather we must allow the Holy Spirit to lead us. Romans 8:14 states that as many as are led by the Spirit of God these are the sons of God.

Whilst God has promised you His spirit, it is your duty to receive this promise by faith and ensure that once you have received Him you do not let Him leave. For God's promise is for yourself, your children and your family. Remember, if you want to go the distance, you need the Holy Spirit to help you. I pray that you will be led at all times by the Holy Spirit so that you can receive and retain all of God's blessings.

The Holy Spirit is given for the benefit of all and not just for the individual who receives Him.

Chapter 3

God's Promises are Sure

God's promises are yea and amen, when God promises a blessing He stands by His Word. When God makes a promise to you despite it taking time to manifest, He will bring it to pass. Men do not have the power to change or alter God's promises concerning your life. Balaam attested to the goodness and faithfulness of God when he was asked by Balak to curse the children of Israel, he stated that God had blessed the children of Israel whom He had chosen to be His children and He would not renegade from His promises to them (*Numbers 23: 19-20*).

'For as many as are the promises of God, they all find their Yes [answer] in Him [Christ]. For this reason we also utter the Amen (so be it) to Go through Him [in His Person and by His agency] to the glory of God'—2 Corinthians 1:20 (AMP).

What does the word 'promise' really mean for us in the context of what God is saying? Do we really understand its meaning?

The Free English Dictionary.com defines 'Promise' as:

A)—(noun)

- A declaration assuring that one will or will not do something; a vow.
- Something promised.
- Indication of something favourable to come; expectation: a promise of spring in the air.

B)—(verb)

- promised, promising, promises
- To commit oneself by a promise to do or give; pledge; left but promised to return.
- To make a declaration assuring that something will or will not be done.
- To afford a basis for expectation: an enterprise that promises well.

You can see from the above definitions that the word promise includes giving a declaration that something will or will not be done and/or to commit oneself by a promise. This is exactly what happens when God makes a promise to you, by His declaration He assures you that what He has promised to do for you He will do.

When Joshua distributed the land given by God to the children of Israel, he thanked God for keeping His promises to them and giving them the land that He had promised to their forefathers. Joshua also thanked God for not allowing their enemies to overcome them and for fulfilling every single word that He had spoken concerning them (*Joshua 21: 43-45*).

Our God is a faithful God; He keeps His promises and stands by His word to ensure that every word He has spoken does not fall to the ground. God is not like men who lie; when God promises a blessing He honours His Word. When Joseph interpreted the Chief Butler's dream, he promised Joseph that when he was restored by Pharaoh to his position he would remember him, the Butler however failed to remember Joseph who spent a further two years in prison. God remembered His promise of blessings to Joseph and set Him free to walk into his inheritance (*Genesis 40:1—41:14*). You need to depend upon God for your promotion, as your promotion does not come from the east, west or south but from the Lord (*Psalms 75:6-7*).

Promises God Made in the Bible

1. God's Promise of Man's Restoration—(Genesis 3:15)

At the fall of man in Genesis, God promised to put an enmity between the woman and satan and that the woman's offspring (Jesus Christ) would bruise and tread his (satan's) head underfoot. He also promised to restore man back to his rightful place in Him (*Romans 8*).

> *'And I will put enmity between you and the woman, and between your seed and her Seed; He shall bruise your head, and you shall bruise His heel" (Genesis 3:15).*

When Jacob (Israel) was about to die, he called all his children together and blessed them, he told each son what he would become in the future. When it came to Judah's turn to be blessed, Jacob prophesied that out of Judah would come leaders and rulers and that the staff of leadership would not depart until Shiloh (Messiah) came, (*Genesis 49:10-11*). Judah probably did not understand the magnitude of Jacob's blessing on his life and future generations at the time.

God revealed His promise of Restoration to:

a. **Prophet Isaiah** – Prophet Isaiah was shown revelations about the coming of the 'One' (Jesus Christ) that would crush satan's head and restore man back to God (*Isaiah 7:14; 9:6-7*). God also told Prophet Isaiah that the virgin shall give birth to a son and His name shall be called Immanuel — God is with us.
b. **Prophet Micah** — Prophet Micah was given a revelation of the coming of the 'One' (Jesus Christ) who would redeem man back to God (*Micah 5:2-5*).
c. **Joseph (Jesus' earthly father)** – when Mary was pregnant with Jesus an angel of the Lord appeared to Joseph in his dream and told him that the child Mary was carrying will be the Saviour (*Matthew 1: 20-21*).

Jesus Christ was born according to prophecies given; He died on the cross for the sins of mankind. He confirmed that His God-given assignment was to seek and save those who are lost.

God kept His promise to restore mankind back to Himself despite the passage of time that had elapsed between when the Word was given and its manifestation. In due season God sent His Son, the descendant of Adam and Eve to purchase man's freedom and to reconcile man back to Himself.

'But when the proper time had fully come, God sent His Son, born of a woman, born subject to [the regulations of] the Law, To purchase the freedom of (to ransom, to redeem, to atone for) those who were subject to the Law, that we might be adopted and have Sonship conferred upon us [and be recognized as God's sons]' (Galatians 4:4-5 (Amp).

2. God's Promises to Abraham—(Genesis 12-22)

God first appeared to Abram when he was seventy-five years old and living in Haran. He told Abram to change his location (*Genesis 12*). God also appeared to Abram when he was ninety-nine years old, and He promised to bless him and his descendants. He promised to give him a son who would be called Isaac. God promised to establish His covenant with him and to give him and his descendants the land of Canaan. God changed his name to Abraham and his wife's name to Sarah to reflect the coming blessings. God started small with him and later multiplied his descendants. The Lord asked Abraham if there was anything too hard or difficult for Him to do.

"Therefore Sarah laughed to herself, saying, After I have become aged shall I have pleasure and delight, my lord (husband), being old also? And the Lord asked Abraham, Why did Sarah laugh, saying, Shall I really bear a child when I am so old? Is anything too hard or too wonderful for the Lord? At the appointed time, when the season [for her delivery] comes around, I will return to you and Sarah shall have born a son" Genesis 18:12-14 (Amp).

God appeared to Abraham at intervals to reiterate His promises to him. It took almost twenty-five years for the manifestation of the promise. God fulfilled His promise to Abraham when he was 100 years old by giving him a son (Isaac) through Sarah, despite his impatience by sleeping with Hagai, his wife's handy maid and having a son named Ishmael through her (*Genesis 16*). The consequences of Abraham's actions were costly, as disunity and jealousy took hold in his home resulting in him sending Hagai and Ishmael away to create peace with his wife (*Genesis 21*). Taking matters into our own hands can only lead to confusion, the consequences of which may last a lifetime. By performing "Plan B" we are telling God that we do not believe Him and His Word.

Stop trying to assist God for His Hands are not short.

Unlike Abraham, Job did not take matters into his own hands when he was faced with setbacks and challenges, rather he waited until his change came. He said, "*If a man dies, shall he live again? All the days of my warfare and service I will wait, till my change and release shall come" (Job 14:14—Amp).*

You must wait like Job did for your victory to come forth as God will fight your cause and bring to pass what He has promised. Do not allow unbelief or impatience rob you of God's blessings. If God has promised you that your unbelieving husband/partner will be saved or that your sick husband/partner or child will be healed, hold on to this promise until the change you want to see comes to pass, for with God all things are possible.

As you are Abraham's child by faith in God you are destined to become great by reason of God's covenant with him. God's irrevocable and unconditional covenant with Abraham means that:

A. Your life is blessed:

1) You have physical strength and agility — Abraham lived to a good old age, satisfied and satiated so likewise would you.
2) Financially — You will never lack or be deprived of any good thing.
3) Mentally — You will have sound mental acumen; you would stand before men and display unequalled comprehension, wisdom and understanding.
4) Spiritually — You will have a discerning heart and will be drawn to the things of the Spirit.

B. Your family is blessed:

By reason of God's everlasting and eternal covenant with Abraham your family is also blessed as God's covenant of blessing extends to them.

C. Whoever blesses you will be blessed and whoever curses you will be cursed:

God promised Abraham that He would bless whosoever blesses him and curse whosoever curses him. The same covenant applies to you today, whosoever chooses to bless you God will bless, but whosoever chooses to curse you will be cursed. May you continue to walk in this promise!

3) God's Promise to Isaac—(Genesis 17:19)

Isaac was both Abraham's and Sarah's promised son with whom God had established His covenant of peace and posterity. God's promise of generational blessings did not end with Abraham but perpetrated downwards to his son, Isaac.

> *'But God said, Sarah your wife shall bear you a son indeed, and you shall call his name Isaac [laughter]; and I will establish My covenant or solemn pledge with him for an everlasting covenant and with his posterity after him' (Genesis 17:19—Amp).*

When Isaac grew up he married Rebekah who had twin boys for him (Esau and Jacob). When there was famine in the land Isaac took his family to Gerar, to Abimelech, King of the Philistines. God appeared to Isaac there and told him not to go down to Egypt but to dwell temporarily in the land. God promised to favour him with blessings. God promised to bless his descendants and to give him all the lands, which He had promised Abraham; in obedience Isaac remained in the land and planted and sowed his seed and he received a hundred-fold return. The Lord blessed him abundantly.

> *"Then Isaac sowed seed in that land and received in the same year a hundred times as much as he had planted, and the Lord favoured him with blessings. And the man became great and gained more*

and more until he became very wealthy and distinguished" (Genesis 26:12-13—Amp).

Isaac listened to God's counsel for his life and remained in the land and reaped a hundred-fold return on what he had sown. As a result of God's promise, Isaac became great, very wealthy and distinguished.

My prayer is that as you continue to obey God in all your ways that He will continue to fulfil His promises to you resulting in your greatness.

4) God's Promise to Jacob—(Genesis 28-46)

God's promise transcended generations and it flowed downwards to Jacob. When Isaac was old and almost blind, he called Esau and asked him to go into the open country to hunt game and prepare food for him to eat so that he could pronounce his paternal blessings on him. Whilst he was gone, Rebekah asked Jacob to deceive Isaac so that the paternal blessing can be bestowed upon him instead of Esau, his twin brother. Jacob cooked the meal suggested by his mother and gave it to Isaac to eat, after eating the meal Isaac pronounced God's blessings on him. Isaac said:

'And may God give you of the dew of the heavens and of the fatness of the earth and abundance of grain and [new] wine; Let peoples serve you and nations bow down to you; be master over your brothers, and let your mother's sons bow down to you. Let everyone be cursed who curses you and favoured with blessings who blesses you' (Genesis 27: 28-29—Amp).

When Esau heard what Jacob had done and that Isaac had blessed Jacob he cried and begged his father to bless him as well. Although Isaac blessed him, he was told that he and his descendant's would perpetually serve Jacob's descendants until he broke Jacob's yoke from off his neck and that there would be enmity between himself and Jacob's descendants. This prophecy came to pass when Esau's descendants — the Amelekites — obstructed Jacob's descendants — the Israelites — when they fled from Egypt at Rephidim (*Exodus 17:8*) and the Edomites refused to allow the Israelites pass through their land at Kadesh (*Numbers 20:14-21*). I pray that you will not be faced with a situation where you are so desperate that you decide to help God perform His promises.

This is proof that you should not follow the popular adage that says, "Heaven helps those who help themselves", as this is not scriptural.

After Jacob received Isaac's blessings he left for Padan-aran (Haran) to his mother's people because Esau wanted to kill him. On his way he came to a place where he stayed for the night, he fell into a deep sleep and had a dream. God appeared to him in this dream and promised to give him and his descendants the place where he was laying. God promised to make his descendents numerous as the sand and that all the families of the earth will be blessed because of him. God promised to bless him, to keep him safe, to take care of him and to bring him back to the place where he was laying. When Jacob awoke from his dream, he called the place **Bethel** and said if God keeps His promises of bringing him back to **Bethel he would make the Lord his God**.

Jacob subsequently married his Uncle's (Laban) daughters Leah and Rachel. In the course of time, the Lord blessed Jacob with eleven sons and one daughter whom his two wives and their two maids bore him. After the birth of his eleventh son (Joseph) he decided to return home, for he was exceedingly blessed—he had many goats, sheep, camels, donkeys, menservants and maid servants causing both his uncle and his sons to be jealous of him. The Lord appeared to Jacob and told him to return to his people, as He would be with him. Jacob called his family and collected all his belongings and left for the **land of Canaan, to Isaac his father**.

Jacob sent messengers and gifts ahead of him to Esau in order to pacify him for stealing his birthright several years before; he also sent his wives, maids and children ahead of him. During his night season, a man wrestled with him till daybreak and when the man saw that it was daylight and he had not prevailed against Jacob he touched Jacob's thigh causing it to dislodge. Jacob held unto the man and refused to release him until the man blessed him. It was at this stage that the man told him that he would no longer be called Jacob but Israel (contender with God). Jacob called that place Peniel. God later told Israel (Jacob) to go to **Bethel** and dwell there and to build Him an altar because He had fulfilled His promise of bringing him back safely. Israel went to Bethel with his family and possessions and built an altar to the Lord there in thanksgiving.

God then appeared to Israel (Jacob) again and renewed His covenant to bless him and to give him the land that He had promised his fathers Abraham and Isaac. In the course of time there was famine in the land, God told Israel to go down to Egypt and to Joseph. Whilst on his way to Egypt God met him at Beersheba and renewed His promises to him, God told him not to fear going down to Egypt because He would make him a great nation there; God promised to bring him out of Egypt and that Joseph, his son would close his eyes in his death (*Genesis 46*). Jacob (Israel) lived for seventeen years in Egypt and died at the age of 147 years.

You can see from Jacob's (Israel) life that God promised to bless, keep and protect him and to be with him always; God promised to keep him safe and to bring him back to the land he was sleeping on (Bethel); to give that land to his descendants, and to make his offspring as the dust or sand of the ground (uncountable) and that through him the families of the earth would be blessed. God kept His promises, leading Jacob to build an altar to Him when he returned to the land of Bethel. Jacob's journey took him over twenty years. When God promises you a thing, He will surely bring it to pass, as His Word stands forever.

You must understand that when God makes a promise to bless you, between the time the word is given and the manifestation of His Word there will be trying and bumpy times, but God will give you the victory in the end. **God's Word and promises to you are settled**, He does not take His Word to you lightly and His promises will come to pass, no matter how long it takes.

'The grass withers, the flower fades, But the word of our God stands forever" Isaiah 40:8.

5) God's Promise to Joseph—(Genesis 37-42)

Joseph was the eleventh child of Jacob (Israel) and first son of Rachel. As the child of Jacob's old age Jacob loved him more than his other children and made him a coat (tunic) with sleeves, when Joseph's siblings saw this they were jealous. When Joseph had a dream and told his brothers about it, they hated him for it. When he told them yet another dream that he saw the eleven stars, sun, and moon bow down to him, his brothers could not take it any longer. When he told his father about his dream, his father (Jacob) asked him if indeed his mother, brothers and himself would bow down to him and his father pondered over his dreams.

His father understood that Joseph would be blessed far above any member of his family. Joseph also understood that he was going to be blessed far above his siblings, however because of his naivety, he gloated to his brothers about it. His brothers were angry that God had destined to bless Joseph above them. Because of their jealousy, they planned to kill him and cast him into a pit but Reuben persuaded them not to do so instead they sold him to the Ishmaelites for twenty pieces of silver and the Ishmaelites in turn sold him to Potiphar, an officer of Pharaoh, in Egypt.

The Lord prospered Potiphar's house because of Joseph resulting in Potiphar placing him in charge of all his possessions. Here you begin to see the manifestation of God's blessings on Joseph. When Joseph refused Potiphar's wife's sexual advances, she cried rape and Joseph was cast into the king's prison. Whilst in prison because of God's Hands on his life he was placed in charge of all the other prisoners by the prison warden.

Whilst in prison, Joseph interpreted the dreams of the Chief Butler and Baker and their dreams came to pass as predicted, Joseph told both the Butler and Baker to mention him to Pharaoh but they forgot about him. Two years later Pharaoh had a dream and there was no one to interpret it for him, the Chief Butler suddenly remembered Joseph. Joseph was brought out of the prison, shaved and given new clothes. Joseph interpreted Pharaoh's dreams and he was made governor and put in charge of Egypt. Because Pharaoh's dreams related to periods of abundance and famine in Egypt, Joseph was placed in charge of storing food and grain for the years of famine (*Genesis 40 and 41*). Pharaoh gave Joseph an Egyptian wife who later bore him two sons called Manasseh and Ephraim. Joseph was thirty years old when he came before Pharaoh, by this time he had spent thirteen years in Egypt as he was only seventeen years old when he was sold into slavery.

When Jacob heard that there was grain in Egypt he sent his ten sons to Egypt to buy grain, as there was famine in his land. When they got to Egypt they bowed before Joseph but they did not recognise him even though he recognised them. Joseph asked them questions about their father and brother Benjamin. Later, he identified himself to them. Joseph's brothers returned home and told their father that Joseph was still alive, well and richly blessed. They saw the manifestation of Joseph's dream before their very eyes. Joseph held a feast for them on their arrival. He told his brothers not to be distressed as God had sent him down to Egypt for a purpose ahead of them, although they had meant it for evil, God had turned it around for his good.

> *'Then Joseph could not restrain himself before all those who stood by him, and he cried out, "Make everyone go out from me!" So no one stood with him while Joseph made himself known to his brothers. And he wept aloud, and the Egyptians and the house of Pharaoh heard it. Then Joseph said to his brothers, "I am Joseph; does my father still live?" But his brothers could not answer him, for they were dismayed in his presence. And Joseph said to his brothers, "Please come near to me." So they came near. Then he said, "I am Joseph your brother, whom you sold into Egypt. But now, do not therefore be grieved or angry with yourselves because you sold me here; for God sent me before you to preserve life. For these two years the famine has been in the land, and there are still five years in which there will be neither plowing nor harvesting. And God sent me before you to preserve a posterity for you in the earth, and to save your lives by a great deliverance. So now it was not you who sent me here, but God; and He has made me a father to Pharaoh, and lord of all his house, and a ruler throughout all the land of Egypt' (Genesis 45:1-8).*

Joseph sent for his family and father to come down to Egypt. Jacob and his family joined Joseph in Egypt and Pharaoh gave them the land of Goshen. **In accordance with God' promise**, Joseph now took care of his siblings, father and entire household. Jacob saw the manifestation of God's promises to him, He blessed Joseph before dying at the age of 110 years. When the children of Israel finally left Egypt after God had delivered them from bondage they took Joseph's bones with them and buried him in Shechem, in the piece of land that Jacob had bought according to the undertaking made by his brethren (*Genesis 46-50; Exodus 13:19*).

You can see from Joseph's life that succeeding in life sometimes involves being **confident in God that He who has started a good**

work in you is able to bring it to perfect completion. Trust God to make the journey with you all the way; do not allow doubt or unbelief to rob you of the blessings that God has promised you.

'Being confident of this very thing, that He who has begun a good work in you will complete it until the day of Jesus Christ' (Philippians 1:6).

We can see that Joseph's character was tried and tested and he was not found wanting as he did not give into fornication, bitterness or un-forgiveness.

Leave all your hurts, pains and disappointments in God's hands and see what miracles God will bring about in your life. You must hold on to God like Joseph did for the manifestation of God's promises to you.

6) God's Promise of Deliverance to the Children of Israel—(Genesis 15:13-16)

God visited the children of Israel at varying times to promise them that He would deliver them out of captivity. He promised Israel that at the time of reckoning, their captors would be punished for enslaving them. God continually told Israel that He would take them out of captivity into a land flowing with milk and honey (Canaan) as He had promised their fore-fathers, Abraham, Isaac and Jacob (Israel). God had told Abraham that his descendants would go to a foreign land (Egypt) where they would be slaves for 400 years but that He would bring judgement on that land for holding them in slavery. He said at the appointed time He would bring them out and take them into the Promised Land (Canaan). God kept His promises of deliverance despite the lengthy passage of time — 400 years.

'Then He said to Abram: "Know certainly that your descendants will be strangers in a land that is not theirs, and will serve them, and they will afflict them four hundred years. And also the nation whom they serve I will judge; afterward they shall come out with great possessions. Now as for you, you shall go to your fathers in peace; you shall be buried at a good old age. But in the fourth generation they shall return here, for the iniquity of the Amorites is not yet complete" (Genesis 15:13-16).

When Israel was held captive in Egypt, God told Moses that He had seen Israel's affliction and bondage and that He would bring them out of Egypt with His outstretched arm and by mighty acts of judgement. He hardened Pharaoh's heart and caused Pharaoh to know that He IS GOD. He brought ten plagues on the people of Egypt, at the tenth plague (death of the first born of the Egyptians from that born to man to animals) Pharaoh thrust the people of Israel out of Egypt in fulfilment of God's promise of deliverance. The Israelites did not go empty handed; rather they stripped the Egyptians of their possessions in fulfilment of God's promises of prosperity (*Exodus 7-12*).

When God promises to deliver you, believe that He would do so, no matter how impossible the situation seems.

Has God promised to deliver you out of that financial, spiritual or emotional mess? Hold on to God until your change comes and do not let the devil or unbelief steal God's promises to you. Isaiah 30: 19-20 says that you who dwell in Zion will weep no more for God will be gracious to you at the sound of your cry. Although the Lord has given you the bread of adversity and water of affliction, He will no longer hide Himself from you. You must understand that your challenges are for a short time only and at the appointed time, whatever is holding you down and back will have to let you go.

Our God loves us with an everlasting love and He will never forget us, He will rebuild the waste deserts in our lives and give us a better future (*Jeremiah 31:1-14*). He will restore to us all that has been lost — the years, dreams and hopes that we once had. God promises us freedom from captivity. He says that He would deliver us from the mighty and from those who have a lawful basis for holding us as prey. Isaiah 49:24-26 records that God said that even the lawful captives will be freed from the clutches of the mighty. You might have been held in bondage due to legal rules, ignorance or servitude, God says He will make your captors and oppressors drink their own blood and eat their own flesh. Those who think they can darken your day will be shocked to discover that they will be strangled with the same rope they had used around your neck. **Your day of deliverance is at hand.**

7) God's Promise to David that his Descendants would sit on his Throne forever—*(2 Samuel 7)*

When God rejected Saul as King, He instructed Samuel to anoint David as king. After his ordination, David was anointed two more times by Samuel before he could sit on the throne that God had ordained him to seat upon (*1 Samuel 16; 2 Samuel 7*). David then went about his business, awaiting God's promise. He went out against his enemies and God gave him victory over them. After the Lord had given him rest from his surrounding enemies David desired to build God a Temple. God appeared to Prophet Nathan in the night and told him to tell David that He would bless David and give him an offspring who would build a house for Him and that His kingdom and throne would be established forever, (2 *Samuel 7*). When David received this promise from the Lord he went in before God to thank Him for His goodness, mercy and faithfulness. He felt honoured to be thought of so greatly by God.

God visited Solomon after David's death and renewed His covenant, which He had made with David. God however warned Solomon that if he turned away from following Him that He would cast Israel and the Temple out of His sight (*1 Kings 9:1-10*). Along the way Solomon married many foreign wives and took many concubines who made him worship their idols and forsake God. The Lord warned him about his ways but he refused to listen and change. God tore the kingdom away from him and gave it to his servant but left one tribe to his descendant for David's sake and for the sake of Jerusalem, which He had chosen (*1 Kings 11:29-36 Amp*). When God promised David that his offspring (seed) would sit on his throne forever, He had in mind Jesus Christ, who would sit on David's throne and reign forever until all His enemies are put under His feet.

'For I have said, "Mercy shall be built up forever; Your faithfulness You shall establish in the very heavens." "I have made a covenant with My chosen, I have sworn to My servant David: 'Your seed I will establish forever, And build up your throne to all generations . . ."
(Psalms 89:2-4).

Even when the children of Israel sinned and were sent into captivity, the tribe of Judah was still preserved and God renewed His promises through Zerubbabel son of Shealtiel (*Hagai 2:23*), a descendant of David, that David's son (the Messiah) would sit on David's throne forever (*Matthew 1:11-23*). After Jesus' death and resurrection He stated to His disciples that all authority had been given Him by God in heaven and earth (*Matthew 28:18*). Jesus' pronouncement was in fulfilment of God's promises to David and Prophet Isaiah. Jesus Christ declared himself as the root and offspring of David (*Revelation 22:16*).

"So all the generations from Abraham to David are fourteen, from David to the Babylonian exile (deportation) fourteen generations, from the Babylonian exile to the Christ fourteen generations" (Matthew 1: 17—Amp).

You can see that although God made a promise to David that He would cause his offspring (seed) to sit on his throne forever, David's descendants did not always keep their part of the bargain. However, despite their sin, God kept His own Word; Jesus Christ remains seated on the Throne of King David forever.

When God makes a promise to you, He intends to keep His own side of the bargain; often times we are the ones who cause the fulfilment of God's blessing to be delayed. You must **not allow sin or disobedience to delay God's promises from coming to pass in your life**; neither must you allow your family to hinder the fulfilment of God's promises to you.

8) God's Promises to the Believer—

God makes numerous promises to us as believers, which He intends to keep because we are His children. He promises to bless and keep us, provided we remain in Him. We have to individually keep our part of the agreement in order to see God's promises manifested in our lives.

a) God Promises to be Your Father:

God promises to be your father at all times, He states that you need not feel alone or secluded as He will always be there for you. Even when your parents, family or friends forsake you, He states that He will be there for you.

"'I will be a Father to you, and you shall be my sons and daughters, says the LORD Almighty' (II Corinthians 6:18).

b) God Promises You a New Life in Christ:

God promises to wash all your sins away when you confess your sins and accept Jesus Christ as your personal Lord and saviour,

He promises to give you a new beginning in Christ. There is no need for you to languish in sin or think that you have done so much wrong that there is no way out, Christ is calling you today to Himself and He promises to forgive you and give you a new lease of life.

'Therefore, if anyone is in Christ, he is a new creation; old things have passed away; behold, all things have become new' (II Corinthians 5:17).

c) God Promises Direction for Your Life:

God promises to order your footsteps and direct you in the way that you should go so that you will no longer work in the dark or lead your life by chance (*Proverbs 14:12*). To receive God's guidance and direction for your life you must place your trust and confidence in Him.

'Trust in the LORD with all your heart; and lean not on your own understanding; In all your ways acknowledge Him, And He shall direct your paths' (Proverbs 3:5-6).

d) God Promises to Bless the Works of Your Hands:

When God created you He pronounced His covenant of fruitfulness upon you, He therefore expects you to be fruitful, to multiply and replenish the earth. He does not expect you to be barren in any area of your life. God says that if you diligently hearken to His voice and be watchful to do all His commandments, that He would place you high above every situation and circumstance that comes your way; His blessings will overtake you.

He promises to bless you in your business and finances, however in order for you to obtain these blessings you must open your hands to receive them.

e) God Promises to Supply All Your Needs:

God promises to supply all your needs including your spiritual, housing, financial, social, marital and health needs. He is able to supply all your needs without exception.

'And my God shall supply all your need according to His riches in glory by Christ Jesus' (Philippians 4:19).

'Blessed be the God and Father of our Lord Jesus Christ, who has blessed us with every spiritual blessing in the heavenly places in Christ' (Ephesians 1:3).

f) God Promises You Long Life:

God promises to give you long life and old age. He states that neither you nor your children would die young. He promises to give you long life and carry you when you are old.

'Even to your old age, I am He, and even to gray hairs I will carry you! I have made, and I will bear; Even I will carry, and will deliver you' (Isaiah 46:4).

g) God Promises to give You His Joy and Peace:

God promises to give you inner peace so that you can stay calm when the wind is blowing and all hell has broken loose around you. He states that you will have peace like a river; He promises to give you a reason to laugh so that you can break forth with singing and dancing. Are you praying for the fruit of the womb; a life partner or for success in that business deal? God's peace will garrison your heart while you wait for His answers.

"For you shall go out with joy, And be led out with peace; The mountains and the hills Shall break forth into singing before you, And all the trees of the field shall clap their hands (Isaiah 55: 12).

h) God Promises You Restoration:

God promises to restore everything stolen from you by people and the lost years taken away by satan.

"So I will restore to you the years that the swarming locust has eaten; The crawling locust, the consuming locust, And the chewing locust, My great army which I sent among you' (Joel 2:25).

God also promises to give you a double portion of His Honour and blessing in place of the shame, reproach and dishonour you have endured in the past. He is a restorer of dignity, fortune and hope.

"Instead of your [former] shame you shall have a twofold recompense; instead of dishonour and reproach [your people] shall rejoice in their portion. Therefore in their land they shall possess double [what they had forfeited]; everlasting joy shall be theirs." (Isaiah 61:7).

i) God Promises to give You Victory over Your Enemies:

God promises to give you victory over every attack of your enemies and those who come against you. He promises you that all weapons formed against you would be destroyed, that even when your enemies gather against you they would fall for your sake.

'No weapon formed against you shall prosper, and every tongue which rises against you in judgment You shall condemn. This is the heritage of the servants of the LORD; And their righteousness is from Me, says the Lord' (Isaiah 54:17).

j) God Promises You Victory over Fear:

You need not fear what tomorrow will bring as God states that He has taken care of your tomorrow. When difficult and challenging situations or circumstances come against you do not fear as God states that He is holding you by your right hand and He has called you by your name.

'For I, the LORD your God, will hold your right hand, saying to you, 'Fear not, I will help you.'(Isaiah 41:13).

'But now, thus says the LORD, who created you, O Jacob, And He who formed you, O Israel: " Fear not, for I have redeemed you; I have called you by your name; You are Mine' (Isaiah 43:1).

k) God promises you Victory over the Power of Death:

You need not fear death or dying as God promises to give you eternal life through Jesus Christ. He has promised to prepare a place for you with Him. Jesus Christ defeated satan and took the keys of Hades from him and so Jesus Christ has conquered the power of death on your behalf.

'But God will redeem my soul from the power of the grave, For He shall receive me' (Selah Psalm 49:15).

l) God Promises to Give us His Silver and Gold:

God promises that our latter days shall be better than our beginning. He says he will give us His peace with His prosperity (*Haggai 2:8-9*). He promises to bless us and to make us profitable in the land in which He has placed us.

Additional Promises for the Believer In Christ

When a person gives their life to Jesus Christ they become a new person in Christ and they have additional blessings bestowed upon them by God. Although you received blessings as Abraham's descendant, the blessings you receive in Christ far outweigh those you receive through Abraham. Some of these additional blessings are:

1) Direct Access to God—

Through Jesus Christ you have direct access to the Father. You become qualified to call upon God because of His beloved Son; He will heed your voice when you call out to Him.

'For through Him we both have access by one Spirit to the Father' (Ephesians 2:18).

2) Adoption by God—

You become a joint heir with Christ of God's blessings. As a rightful heir, you become entitled to the privileges and entitlements of a son who has come of age.

'Having predestined us to adoption as sons by Jesus Christ to Himself, according to the good pleasure of His will' (Ephesians 1:5).

'. . . If children, then heirs—heirs of God and joint heirs with Christ, if indeed we suffer with Him, that we may also be glorified together' (Romans 8:17).

3) Inheritance through Christ—

You have a godly inheritance in God through Christ Jesus. You become entitled to inherit the nations as your possessions. He promises us that our offspring would be like the sand and our descendants like the offspring of the sea and their names would never be cut off from Him (*Isaiah 48:17-19*).

'In Him also we have obtained an inheritance, being predestined according to the purpose of Him who works all things according to the counsel of His will' (Ephesians 1:11).

4) **Priesthood –**

You become sanctified as a priest in the order of God. You become set apart for God's kingdom.

'But you are a chosen generation, a royal priesthood, a holy nation, His own special people, that you may proclaim the praises of Him who called you out of darkness into His marvellous light' (1 Peter 2: 9).

'and He has made us king and priests to His God and Father, to Him be glory and dominion forever and ever. Amen' (Revelation 1:6).

The promises given by God in the Bible are meant for everyone and not just a selected few. As a descendant of Abraham and co-heir with Jesus Christ you must lay claim to these promises by faith in Christ so that you can take your rightful place in the Kingdom of God.

As I close this chapter, I pray that **nothing will keep you from taking hold of God's promises** today in Jesus' name. Amen.

Chapter 4

God's Blessings Are For Today

Yesterday's blessings can become an obstacle in your life if you dwell too long at the door of past successes. You need to shake yourself and move on to take hold of all that God has in store for you and not procrastinate or be fearful as 'Today' is your day of deliverance and not tomorrow.

In Deuteronomy 9, God tells the children of Israel through Moses that it was time for them to cross over the River Jordan to disposes all their enemies of God's blessings, which their enemies were holding on to. God used the word 'Today' to signify the urgency of the matter as the children of Israel had stayed too long in the mountains and had become accustomed to it, they were not too keen in moving forward as they had become complacent and comfortable with their current position.

In order for us to fully appreciate the gravity of the word '**Today**', let us look at its meaning. **Dictionary.com defines today as:**

Today

- This present day: *Today is beautiful.*
- This present time or age: *the world of today.*
- On this present day: *I will do it today.*

The word 'today' means 'present' rather than 'later' God expects us to act on His Word and receive His blessings immediately. This is certainly the day that God expects us to receive our blessing so we must arise to take hold of it. You must rejoice and be glad for being alive today.

God will go before you today (presently) as a devouring fire, there is no need to fear what the day will bring. God will destroy all that stands as an obstacle before you as it is only God that can prevail against your enemies (*Deuteronomy 20:4*).

> *'Know therefore this day that the Lord your God is He Who goes over before you as a devouring fire. He will destroy them and bring them down before you; so you shall dispossess them and make them perish quickly, as the Lord has promised you' Deuteronomy 9:3 (AMP).*

God promises that wherever our feet treads He will give us and that no man would be able to stand before us (*Deut. 11: 24-25).* After Moses' death, Joshua was faced with the challenge of taking the children of Israel across the River Jordan and into the Promised Land. God appeared to him and told him to take over Moses' mantle. God reiterated the promises that He had given to Moses and told him that wherever the soles of his feet tread that He would give to him just as He had promised Moses (*Joshua 1:3*).

When the children of Israel were defeated at the battle of Ai, the people were distraught; Joshua and the elders of Israel rent their clothes and laid on the ground before the Ark of the Lord from morning until evening, they put dust on their heads and wept before the Lord. God appeared to Joshua and told him to get up from lying on his face. He wanted Joshua to take action by punishing the wrongdoer in the camp. By lying down, nothing happened, no significant changes occurred. However, by acting on God's promptings the wrongdoer was brought to justice (*Joshua 7:10-14; 8*).

God intended to bless the children of Israel by giving them victory over the people of Ai, but they had allowed their flow of blessings to be blocked because of their sin; Joshua and the elders of Israel did not help matters by lying on their faces. Joshua rose up to confront the sin in Israel's midst, you too should rise up to address your issues and move on so that you do not postpone the day of your blessings. Stop looking back.

He [God] does not say come tomorrow, next week or next year, He states that you should come now (today).

When challenging situations come our way it is often easy to forget God and resort to having a pity party. Do not let difficult situations prevent you from immediately dealing with challenges, as God has promised to fight in your corner and give you the victory you desire. You may have tried reasoning your way out of difficult situations but found that this has not solved the problem. God states that you should come now (**today**) to Him so that you can argue your case and reason together to find the solutions you are looking for, according to His Word.

The hardest part is starting what you have promised yourself you would do; so the best way to overcome this challenge is to schedule goals with a set timescale so that you have no choice but to complete the task.

In order to take hold of the blessings God has promised, we need to understand the immediacy of the Word given. We should accept every Word given to us by faith and not allow unbelief to steal our blessings.

In 2 Kings 7:1-2, the captain on whose hand the king leaned upon doubted and made jest of the word of God spoken through Prophet Elisha, he had said that even if God opened the windows of Heaven, the blessings promised by God could not satisfy the needs of the people. Prophet Elisha told him that he would see the blessings with his own eyes but that he would not eat of it. When the blessing came the children of Israel trampled on the captain to reach it resulting in his death; he saw the blessing with his own eyes but did not partake of it; on the other hand, four lepers who acted immediately by faith on the word of God received the blessing that was promised. My prayer is that you would not allow unbelief, doubt or worry to rob you of the blessings that you have waited so long for (*2 Kings 7*).

Your Blessings for Today

Sometimes when God promises to bless you and make you a blessing to your nation some unknown enemies reveal themselves to you by opposing you; they try to frustrate God's plans and promises to you; they may even laugh at your slow progress and prophesy that whatever you achieve will result in your mockery by all who see it. **I want you to know that God will frustrate your enemies' plans and prophesies concerning you.** We have to work at the promises God has given us despite the opposition.

You must pursue your goals, dreams and visions immediately despite the opposition that comes against you because God would give you the victory in the end, and all your enemies round about would see your victory and fear your God. You must get up on your feet and not allow circumstances to dictate your progress or cause you to fear because God has not given you a spirit of fear; rather He has given you a spirit of power, love and a sound mind (*2 Timothy 1:7*). You must not allow procrastination to keep you down or prevent you from taking action.

A decade ago, my sister and I were working at places where there were no career development opportunities. A brother in Christ informed us that there were possible openings in his Practice so we should call his practise to arrange an appointment with his employer. The work being offered was ideal for me as it would enable me to meet the requirements for qualifying as a lawyer; however the downside to accepting the job was the pay packet, which was far less than what I was earning at the time. I had a week to confirm whether I would accept the terms of pay or not. I kept putting off making a decision and dissuaded my sister from accepting the job as well. I was aware that there were other candidates interested in the position so we faced the risk of missing out on a good opportunity.

On the day before the deadline, I went shopping for some clothes with my sister. As we made our way up the escalator to one of the stores, my sister turned to me and said she was persuaded that God wanted us to take up the positions in the practice despite the lower pay packet. She said God wanted us to step out in faith even if we had to downsize our lifestyle as God will take care of our bills and living expenses. She said we must not miss the opportunity of seeing God work things out for our good as the job was a blessing from God who had orchestrated things for our benefit. I stood at the top of the escalator and reflected on what she said, I became persuaded that God was in the midst of the situation and He knew what He was doing. I took out my mobile phone and called the Practice, accepting the job immediately.

I had almost allowed indecision; fear and procrastination steal the blessing that God had for me. Not only did I acquire the relevant working experience needed for my qualification, I went on to achieve greater things as the job had a domino effect on other aspects of my life, the job was a blessing in disguise. If I had not allowed the Holy Spirit to guide me into acting diligently, fear would have held me back from pursuing my life's dream. My sister took up a position at the same practise a month afterwards and went on to qualify as a lawyer. She too went on to achieve greater things in Christ.

In Hebrews 3:15, God states that when you hear His voice **today**, you should not harden your heart. He states that you should be receptive to His words and act immediately on it. People often **procrastinate** and/or are lazy when it comes to pursuing their life's dream.

Edward Young an English poet (1683—1765) said that, "Procrastination is the thief of time."

Do you know that you are wasting your time if you keep putting off today what must be done now?

People **procrastinate (delay**) in taking action or put off taking action for different reasons. In order to understand why people procrastinate in taking action, we must first understand what the word 'Procrastination' means.

Dictionary.com defines Procrastination as:

- To defer action; delay: *to procrastinate until an opportunity is lost.*
- To put off till another day or time; defer; delay.

Freedictionary.com states that Procrastination is:

- A type of avoidance behaviour characterised by deferment of actions or tasks to a later time.

Procrastination is the habit of putting things off for tomorrow what can be done today or putting tasks off to the last minute possible when it should be done immediately. Procrastination can be a problem in a person's life, relationships or career and stems from a dysfunctional viewpoint. Psychologists often cite it as a mechanism for coping with the anxiety associated with starting or completing any task or decision.

On one occasion I was in the process of purchasing a property just before the property crash and credit crunch. I wanted a mortgage to complete the purchase of this property but I had been delaying calling my Independent Financial Adviser to arrange the mortgage for me. However I got up on this particular day to deal with this matter as I felt that God was saying I should not procrastinate any longer. I called my Adviser up on the phone and he began to laugh. He told me that I had called just in time that day, because the banks were stopping their offers of giving large advances. He said that if I had not called that day, the banks would have required a deposit of 40% from me to complete the purchase instead of 15% which was the percentage required when the market was good. I placed the phone handset down and knelt to thank God for nudging me into taking action that moment and for giving me the grace to act upon His Voice to my benefit.

Acting **e**xpeditiously on God's Word will result in your financial blessing and security.

Procrastination can be caused by but is not limited to any of the following: http://en.wikibooks.org/wiki/Overcoming_Procrastination/Causes

- Anxiety and fear
- Uncertainty
- Bad habits
- Discouragement

- Frustration
- Fear of failure or fear of success
- Low self esteem
- Addictions
- Disorganisation
- Distractions
- Lack of time management skills
- Lack of self control
- Paranoia
- Arrogance and pride
- Interruptions from visitors, family or friends

Procrastination can lead to the following consequences:
http://en.wikibooks.org/wiki/Overcoming_Procrastination/Consequences

- Financial difficulties—from not paying bills or loans on time; not managing ones finances or monitoring ones bank account/s;
- Lost opportunities—from not attending job interviews on time or at all; not keeping business appointments or not registering that patent/copyright resulting in another person stealing one's ideas;
- Missed deadlines—resulting in loss of friendships or relationships because the person cannot be trusted to keep appointments or carry out actions/work he/she has promised;
- Poor health—due to non commitment in taking one's medication at the right time or at all or not changing ones life style to gain better health such as putting off going for a walk or the gym;
- Unnecessary expenses—arising from inaction such as payment of late fees, overdrawn charges etc;
- Poor performance—arising from failure to put in that extra hour or going the extra mile.

Procrastination can be eliminated by some of the following ways:
http://en.wikibooks.org/wiki/Overcoming_Procrastination/Eliminating_Procrastination

- Changing one's attitude;
- Having a positive mental attitude;
- Focusing one's mind to the tasks at hand and eliminating all distractions;
- Thinking rationally;
- Acquiring self-management skills such as goal setting, planning, scheduling, prioritising, delegation and keeping a journal;
- Planning ahead;
- Taking a step at a time by breaking down major goals into smaller tasks and dealing with each task at a time;
- Changing one's habit of putting things off to the last minute or the next week or the next year;
- Getting back on one's feet after failing and starting again;
- Building on one's strengths;
- Eating healthy and taking care of one's health;
- Praying;
- Asking for the Holy Spirit's help in overcoming the desire of putting things off;
- Being courageous;
- Conducting regular self appraisals;
- Learning to accept positive/justified criticism as this would hold you in good stead;
- Stop worrying unnecessarily;
- Learning to work with others.

All problems, personal, national, or combat, become smaller if you don't dodge them, but confront them. Touch a thistle timidly, and it pricks you; grasp it boldly, and its spines crumble. Carry the battle to the enemy! Lay your ship

alongside his!"
—Admiral William "Bull" Halsey

In Joshua 3:15-17 God did not divide the River Jordan and allow the children of Israel to pass through on dry ground until the feet of those who bore the Ark of the Covenant and the feet of the priests bearing the Ark were in the brink of the water as He had directed them. It was only after they had complied with His instructions that the River Jordan parted into two resulting in the children of Israel passing through on dry ground thereby removing the last obstacle in their path to their entry into the Promised Land (Canaan).

It is imperative to note that **(a)** nothing happened until the men and the priests carrying the Ark stood on the brink of the water and **(b)** as a result of their actions the children of Israel were able to enter into the Promised Land and take hold of their possessions.

You must not run away from tasks facing you, rather you must face them headlong. You must always consider the benefits from completing a task. We need to remain focused on God's assignment and purpose for our lives so that we do not miss opportunities that come our way.

In Proverbs 6:4-11; 12:27 and 20:13, we are told to look at the ants that have no ruler, chief or overseer yet they plan ahead for the winter by storing up abundant food in the summer; likewise we are told to be proactive and not let too much sleep, delaying or inaction steal our blessings. We are told that too much sleep, delaying and inaction leads to poverty because these prevent us from taking hold of the many opportunities that come our way.

When you make a vow or pledge to the Lord, God expects you to honour your word at the set time and not put off paying it. The

Bible states that God has no pleasure in those who defer from honouring their dues.

> *'When you make a vow to God, do not delay to pay it; For He has no pleasure in fools. Pay what you have vowed'* (Ecclesiastes 5:4).

> ***You must not use prayer and hearing from God as an excuse for procrastination.***

When God gives you a word or asks you to do something or refrain from doing something, He expects you to act immediately on His Word, as God does not suffer fools gladly. I am not saying that you mustn't take time to pray and hear from God before taking any decision or taking any action. However, what I am saying is that there must be a balance between praying, planning and action taking. You must not become so spiritually minded that you are of no earthly use or use prayer to bring disrepute to God's name, as those who forever put things off never become successful.

Procrastination also rears its ugly head when one is confronted with the issue of salvation, i.e. where one wants to spend eternity (heaven or hell). We are told in 2 Corinthians 6:2 that today is the day of salvation and in Ecclesiastes 12:1 that we should remember our creator in the days of our youth before the day of evil comes. **If you have not yet given your life to Jesus Christ you must positively and actively do so now (today) as tomorrow may be too late (Proverbs 27:1).**

> *John 3:16 says that, "for God so loved the world, that He gave His begotten Son, that whomsoever believes in Him will not perish but have everlasting life."*

> *Roman 10: 9-10 states that, "that if you confess with your mouth the Lord Jesus and believe in your heart that God has raised Him from the dead, you will be saved. For with the heart one believes*

unto righteousness, and with the mouth confession is made unto salvation."

You can ask Jesus Christ to come into your life now (today); to cleanse your sins away with His Blood, which He shed on the Cross of Calvary; to fill you with His Holy Spirit that He promised you and to transform your life from today onwards. When Jesus Christ comes into your life, your life will never be the same. He will give you a fresh revelation of Himself and His plans for your life. The Holy Spirit will guide and help you to fulfil your purpose in Jesus' Name.

You can say this simple but powerful prayer now—

"I acknowledge that Jesus Christ came to the earth; that He died on the Cross of Calvary for me; that He resurrected and there is power in His resurrection. I believe that He has redeemed me from the penalty of sin and death. I confess all my sins to Him; I ask Him to forgive me now (today), to transform me and to start a new work in my life. I ask you Jesus Christ to come into my life so that I can live my life for you. I thank you Lord Jesus for forgiving me all my sins and giving me eternal life. Amen.

Now that you have given your life to Christ, you must begin to read the Bible daily and pray for the Holy Spirit's guidance and direction. You should ask Him to give you spiritual understanding and enlightenment. You may wish to start reading from the Gospel of John, which explains God's love for mankind and Jesus' willingness to sacrifice Himself so that man (including you) could be reconciled to God. You should also consider finding a local church that is Bible-based if you don't already attend one. You should introduce yourself to the Pastor who will nurture you spiritually and build you up in the Lord. The same applies to those who once attended church but backslid for one reason or another. Return to the Lord and He will return to you.

My prayer is that you will not allow procrastination, slothfulness or fear to prevent you from taking hold of all the blessings that God has in store for you today. As you open your heart to God's leadings and teachings, God will begin to change your mindset about acting promptly. The Holy Sprit will cause you to get up and act now. Your blessing is definitely meant **for today and not for tomorrow**; so rise up and take hold of God's blessings for you today.

Redeem the time! God only knows, how soon our little life may close, With all its pleasures and its woes; Redeem the time!
-Anonymous

Chapter 5

God's Peace & Rest

God's blessings come with **His Peace and Rest** and not sorrow. When we feel fearful, or have sleepless nights over a blessing that comes into our hands or our way we need to check its source. God has bequeathed His peace upon us and He expects us to reach deep inside ourselves and bring it out.

'The blessing of the Lord—it makes [truly] rich, and He adds no sorrow with it . . .' Proverbs 10:22(AMP).

The Bible states that God created the Heavens, the Earth and every living creature including Man in six days and then **rested** on the seventh day after He had finished his work of creation; He then blessed the seventh day and set it apart as His holy day (*Genesis 2: 2-3).*

God told the children of Israel when they were in the Wilderness of Sin to set aside the seventh day as a day of Sabbath (Rest). He told the people to collect manna once every day for six days but that on the sixth day they were to gather twice as much as no manna would be provided on the seventh day because He expected them to rest from their labour (*Exodus 16*).

In Leviticus 25, God told Moses on Mount Sinai that when the children of Israel got to the land that He had promised them that the land must keep a Sabbath to the Lord; that the people were to work the land for six years and in the seventh year they should allow the land to lie fallow as He would provide surplus for them to reap. He told Moses that the fiftieth year should be declared as the year of liberty for it is the year of Jubilee and everyone should return to their ancestral homes. He also stated that bondservants should be set free and property returned to their owners.

In the fortieth year of the Israelites' wanderings in the wilderness, Moses spoke to the children of Israel, he recalled God's promises to them and told them of how their rebellion and sin had caused an eleven days journey from Horeb to Kadesh-barnea on Canaan's border to take them forty years; he reminded them of God's blessings and faithfulness and of His promise to give them 'Rest' when they entered the land that He had promised them (*Deuteronomy 1:2-3; 12:9-10*). He told the people to rejoice before the Lord when they entered that rest (*Deuteronomy 12:12*), after giving his instructions to the Israelites Moses died on Mount Nebo and Joshua succeeded him.

Joshua testified about God's rest that came with His blessings; he stated that God had given them rest on every side.

> *'The LORD gave them rest on every side, just as he had sworn to their forefathers. Not one of their enemies withstood them; the LORD handed all their enemies over to them. Not one of all the Lord's good promises to the house of Israel failed; every one was fulfilled' Joshua 21:44-45(NIV).*

When God used the word **'Rest'** and **'Peace'** He used them in their entire ramifications. To have an idea of what God means when He uses the words 'Rest' and 'Peace' let us look at their definition.

The Free Dictionary defines PEACE as:

- Stillness or silence
- Absence of mental anxiety: *peace of mind*
- Harmony between people or groups
- In a state of harmony or serenity
- Hold or keep one's peace – to keep silent

The Free Dictionary defines REST as:

- Cessation of work, exertion, or activity.
- Peace, ease, or refreshment resulting from sleep or the cessation of an activity.
- Sleep or quiet relaxation.
- Relief or freedom from disquiet or disturbance.
- Mental or emotional tranquillity.
- To be at peace or ease; be tranquil.

You can see from the above definition that **'Rest'** includes peace; relief or freedom from disquiet or disturbance; being in a state of mental or emotional tranquillity. **Peace** itself refers to the absence of mental anxiety. Rest and peace can be used interchangeably. May God give you rest and peace in your spiritual, mental, emotional and physical being; whatever causes you distress or disturbance would be distressed by God.

Frances Ridley Havergal sang the following, which reinforces God's promise of peace and rest:

> *"Upon the Word I rest, Each pilgrim day; This golden staff is best For all the way. What Jesus Christ hath spoken, Cannot be broken!*

Upon the Word I rest, so strong, so sure, So full of comfort blest, So sweet, so pure! The charter of salvation,Faith's broad foundation. Upon the Word I stand! That cannot die! Christ seals it in my hand. He cannot lie! The word that faileth never! Abiding ever! Chorus. The Master hath said it! Rejoicing in this, we ask not for sign or for token; His word is enough for our confident bliss, — The Scripture cannot be broken!"

In the Old Testament, there are numerous examples of God giving His people Rest, one of whom is Ruth—

God gives rest with His blessings!

In the book of Ruth it is stated that when Naomi tried to send her two daughters-in-law away from her, she asked God to grant them a **home** and **Rest** in each of their own husband's houses (*Ruth 1:9*)**.** Ruth however refused to go back to her people (Moabites) and followed Naomi from Moab to Bethlehem of Judah in Israel, because she understood that to find true and lasting rest she had to worship "The One and only True God" whom Naomi worshipped. Naomi introduced her to Boaz whom she later married. Ruth had a son who became the grandfather of King David (and ancestor of Jesus Christ) The women of the land then said to Naomi, 'Blessed be the Lord, Who has not left her without a close kinsman, and that Ruth was better to her than seven sons (*Ruth 4:13-17*).'

We can see that by following the "One True God" Ruth found peace and rest in her new home as God's peace and rest came with His blessing of a husband and son. **A home should be a place of rest and not where war, disorder or commotion reigns.** As with Naomi, you must endeavour to make your home an environment of security and happiness for your friends, family and in-laws where peoples' gifting can be discovered, developed and promoted. God intends both the married person and the singleton to have peace in their home.

God gives rest with His blessings and He intends you to have rest at all times including the trying and difficult times. He asks that you put your trust in Him and lean on Him for strength. He wants you to focus on Him. God states that when you go through the waters, rivers and fires of life they would not overwhelm you because He will be with you.

'When you pass through the waters, I will be with you; And through the rivers, they shall not overflow you. When you walk through the fire, you shall not be burned; Nor shall the flame scorch you' (Isaiah 43:2).

Even if the mountains and hills are moved or shaken under you, God's covenant of peace shall never be taken from you.

'For the mountains shall depart And the hills be removed, But My kindness shall not depart from you, Nor shall My covenant of peace be removed," Says the LORD, who has mercy on you' (Isaiah 54:10).

God's promise of peace also extends to your children . . .

'All your children shall be taught by the LORD, and great shall be the peace of your children' (Isaiah 54:13)

As long as we are in right standing with God, God promises us that He will give us victory over every attack of the enemy. He will nullify every weapon of the enemy and bring them to nothing. In order to access all His promises and blessings we should forsake our evil ways and our unrighteous thoughts; He states that when we return to Him, He would love, pity and have mercy upon us. He states that He knows that our ways and thoughts defer from His, which is why He is calling us back to Himself. He states that we shall go out with joy and be led forth with peace (*Isaiah 55:7-13*).

When we return to Him our testimony and name will change because He shall delight in us (*Isaiah 62:4*).

Having looked at Rest in the Old Testament, what does the New Testament tell us about God's Promises of Rest—

In Matthew 11:28, Jesus said, *"Come to Me, all you who labour and are heavy laden, and I will give you rest' (NIV).* Jesus Christ promises His rest to all those who are burdened with worry and those who have a heavy heart. He promises that they will find ease, relief and refreshment for their souls.

Whenever you feel low in your spirit, depressed or anxious go to Jesus Christ and ask for his Peace for your troubled soul and you will find His peace (rest). God's promises of rest still stands today in the 21st century,

> *Therefore, while the promise of entering His rest still holds and is offered [today], let us be afraid [to distrust it], lest any of you should think he has come too late and has come short of [reaching] it. Hebrews 4: 1 (AMP).*

Hebrews 3 and 4, records that God swore to the Israelites that they would not enter into His rest because of their unbelief and because of His wrath and indignation; we are being warned today not to fall into the same trap of unbelief as the children of Israel did (*Psalms 95:7-11*). We are told to be receptive to God in all our ways; to trust in him and rely on him so that we can enter into the rest He has promised us.

When God promised His rest, He had something better in mind for us than what we know of today. God still has a full and complete Sabbath rest reserved for His people. We are urged to be zealous in order to enter the rest of God, which brings freedom from weariness, pain and labour (*Hebrews 4*).

You may say to yourself, 'I have gone through so much pain in my life; I have been disappointed and taken advantage of; I have faced so much emotional, sexual, physical, financial or spiritual attack and abuse all of my life; I have been attacked because I am a Christian; when abused and attacked I did not respond; I have given all I have to help others and got nothing in return and yet I was misunderstood. I now feel that there is no hope for me; I don't believe I can ever have this peace (rest) of God, joy or gladness of heart which everyone is talking about.'

I want you to know that if any of the above describes your situation, Jesus Christ understands your pain and sorrow as He also went through the same pain at the cross of Calvary. He will certainly come to your cry for help when and if you call out to Him. God promises that His Spirit will rest on you in your time of pain and fiery trials to give you victory over the works of the devil (*Hebrews 2: 14-18*).

God's promises of peace and rest belong to us through Jesus Christ and it is our duty to receive it by faith by asking Him to give us His peace through the knowledge of Himself and of Jesus Christ. We must ask God to lead us by His spirit and we must continue to trust Him to fulfil His promises of peace to us.

'Grace and peace be multiplied to you in the knowledge of God and of Jesus our Lord' (2 Peter1:2).

The decision to accept God's permanent rest lies with the individual; for the person who does not have Christ and has refused to accept Jesus Christ as his/her personal Lord and Saviour, his/her worries will continue into the realm of eternity, as he/she would have no respite from his/her troubles.

'And the smoke of their torment ascends forever and ever; and they have no respite (no pause, no intermission, no rest, no peace) day or night—these who pay homage to the beast and to his image and whoever receives the stamp of his name upon him 'Revelation 14:11(AMP).

However, for the person who has accepted Jesus Christ as his/her personal Lord and Saviour and who has been washed and cleansed with His blood, he/she will not only have rest on this earth but also have the **rest of eternity** to enjoy fellowship with other believers in God's presence.

'Then I heard further perceiving the distinct words of] a voice from heaven, saying, Write this: Blessed (happy, to be envied) are the dead from now on who die in the Lord! Yes, blessed (happy, to be envied indeed), says the Spirit, [in] that they may rest from their labours, for their works (deeds) do follow (attend, accompany) them!' Revelation 14:13 (AMP).

Rest for the Body

As God demarcated a day of rest from all His work, He expects that we too should rest from all our hard labour. He expects us to spend time recuperating so that we will be in the right frame of mind to worship and serve Him. He purposefully set a day of rest aside in which we could relax and seek His face because He knows that if we do not rest we are likely to suffer burnouts, stress or ill health. You may not find it practical to rest on a Saturday or Sunday because of the nature of your profession or job; you can however set a day aside during the week in which you can rest from your labour and recover your strength.

Jesus took time out from the crowd to receive instructions from God. In Mark 9:2-9 Jesus took only Peter, James and John up a mountain where He transfigured Himself before them and met with

Moses and Elijah to discuss His assignment. Jesus Christ equally took time away from the crowd and from His disciples when He went aside alone to pray at Gethsemane to receive strength from God to complete His assignment (*Matthew 26:36-46*).

You must endeavour to take time off alone from your family, friends and the crowd to seek the face of God so that you can receive fresh revelation and instructions from God about your purpose in life and His plans for you.

Ideas for relaxing and/or resting your body: http://www.wikihow.com/Relax

- Finding a quiet place/quiet room to rest
- Taking a holiday or short break
- Soaking yourself in a hot bath
- Relaxing in bed-have a sleep in, treat yourself to breakfast in bed, read a book in bed
- Having 'me time' in which you treat yourself to a nice film and lunch/dinner all by yourself
- Listening to soft music
- Exercising daily—going walking, swimming, running, etc.
- Having a hobby—such as fishing, sewing, knitting, painting, charitable work
- Avoiding people who are always angry or people who complain all the time as these type of people will drain you
- Learning to prioritize your work to avoid burnouts
- Eating healthy food
- Attending Health Spas for a massage, etc.
- Think positively
- Laughing more
- Praying
- Seek medical/spiritual/psychological help if you are having problems resting or unwinding after protracted periods of time.

Rest in God

When you go your own way and exert your own energy trying to make it happen in your own strength you will be worn out, agitated and restless. Man cannot give you true and lasting peace despite their best intentions and promises. You will find true rest in God alone whose rest comes with peace and tranquillity.

Jesus Christ is the Pillar that holds our lives in place. Your foundation needs to be built on Jesus Christ as all other ground is sinking sand. He will not allow your foot to slip. He will make you rest secured in Him. Whilst waiting for your blessings you must be at peace with yourself and God. You must rest in God.

Cast all your cares on God for He cares for you, learn to trust God with what you have placed on Him and refrain from taking back your worries, cares and burdens. God may not answer your prayers and requests in the way that you expect Him to, but know that He is faithful and just. He will always come through for you in His own timing and way.

God wants you to rest but not on your laurels, as past achievements can be a hindrance to your progress. You need to celebrate yesterday's victories and achievements but remember to move on to sail across many more seas. God will certainly come true for you. He will give you His Peace and Rest with His blessings.

"Blessed be the LORD, who has given rest to His people Israel, according to all that He promised. There has not failed one word of all His good promise, which He promised through His servant Moses (1 Kings 8:56).

I sincerely hope that you will enter into God's rest and find peace for your spirit, soul and body, and that God's peace (rest), which surpasses all understanding, will keep your heart and mind through Christ Jesus (*Philippians 4:7*).

Chapter 6

Endless Possibilities With God

When God says that He has given us the ability to do great exploits, He means absolutely nothing is impossible for us to achieve in His Name. When God promises you something, nothing can restrain or thwart it.

"For with God nothing is ever impossible and no word from God shall be without power or impossible of fulfilment" (Luke 1: 37—Amp).

You must dream big, imagine big and attain big, as all things are possible for those who believe in Christ Jesus. For instance, the fact that others have made it in your aspired field does not mean that there is no more room at the top for you. God has blessed you to be fruitful, to multiply, and to increase, so do not take the back seat. God has given you the strength to go all the way. Psalm 29:11 states that the Lord has given you an unyielding and impenetrable strength and that He has blessed you with His peace. **In your journey to achieving endless possibilities receive God's peace today.** Although your beginning may have been small, your latter years will be so awesome that there will be nothing to compare it with (*Job 8:7*).

The world will wonder at all the miracles taking place in your life. Your generation shall praise God because of you and your achievements. God is taking you somewhere awesome, magnificent and glorious as such, you must be prepared for the change that is coming your way.

> *'For You are my hope; O Lord God, You are my trust from my youth and the source of my confidence. Upon You have I leaned and relied from birth; You are He Who took me from my mother's womb and You have been my benefactor from that day. My praise is continually of You. I am as a wonder and surprise to many, but You are my strong refuge. My mouth shall be filled with Your praise and with Your honour all the day' (Psalms 71: 5-8—Amp).*

In order for you to enter into the realm of 'Endless Possibilities', you must ensure that you:

1) Believe God's promises
2) Speak God's promises into existence by use of positive confessions
3) Act upon God's promises
4) Trust God to keep His Word to you
5) Lean on God alone and not on man, as the arm of flesh will fail you
6) Avoid sin
7) Take Godly and Positive action

By doing these you are calling those things, which are not as though they were (*Romans 4:17*). Proverbs 18:21 states that, 'Death and life' *are* in the power of the tongue, by speaking good things about yourself and calling forth into manifestation what you are trusting God for, God will bring them to pass in due season.

The Bible records endless testimonies of people who rose from obscurity to take centre stage in their time and/or emerged to enter realms of possibilities. Some of these people are:—

- **Abraham/Sarah**—God appeared to Abraham and told him that his wife, Sarah will give birth to a child, in her old age. Sarah laughed when she heard the news, but nothing is too hard for our God as Sarah gave birth to a son, Isaac, at God's appointed time. (*See Chapter 3 of this book — God's Promises Are Sure — for more details of God's faithfulness.*)

- **Joseph**—We know the story of Joseph, (*See Chapter 3 of this book*); he went from prison to the palace. Just like Joseph, you too can come out of every form of bondage that has enslaved you to enter the palace prepared for you by God. You too can become a person to be reckoned with in Jesus' name.

- **David**—God brought David from being a sheepherder to being the ordained and chosen King of Israel. He saw in David a man after his own heart; He saw endless possibilities in David so He elevated him to the much-coveted position of royalty. (1 Samuel 16—18).

- **Daniel**—when Nebuchadnezzar, King of Babylon captured Jerusalem, he took the royal and noble children of Israel with him. He told Ashpenaz, the head of his eunuchs to train them so that they could serve him. One of these children was Daniel (also called Belteshazar). Whilst Daniel was in captivity, he acknowledged, worshipped and trusted God to carry out His purpose for his life. He excelled and became irreplaceable. He was promoted by the King because of his ability to interpret dreams and because he proved himself wiser and more knowledgeable than the king's advisers.

Like Joseph, he too went from slavery to the palace (Book of Daniel).

- **Zachariah/Elizabeth**—Elizabeth, the wife of Zachariah gave birth to John, the Baptist when she was old in age. John, the Baptist later became the forerunner of Jesus Christ — a Child of Destiny. His birth was miraculous, as his parents had lost all hope of ever having a child of their own. But God, who remains constantly unchangeable, kept His promise of giving them a child. Elizabeth, who was past child bearing, conceived and carried the child of destiny to full term (*Luke 1: 5-25*).

There are some people in our times that have cut through the barriers of impossibility and risen from obscurity to the limelight. Some of these people are:

- **Nelson Mandela**—born in Transkei on 18th July 1918. A political activist who faced repression and oppression from the apartheid regime in South Africa. He was banned from addressing the public and arrested in 1962 for inciting people to strike. He was convicted and given a term of five years imprisonment. He was later sentenced to life imprisonment for treason and served his sentence in the notorious Robin Island Prison. He was released from prison on 11th February 1990 and continued his mission.

  In 1991, at the first national conference of the ANC in South Africa he was elected President of the ANC. On 10th May 1994 he was inaugurated as the first democratically elected State President of South Africa. He led South Africa as President from May 1994 to June 1999. Determination and courage saw him through. Mandela has received more than 250 awards over four decades, including the 1993

Nobel Peace Prize. You may read more about ex-President Mandela at: http://en.wikipedia.org/wiki/Mandela

- **Barack Obama**—is the 44th President of United States of America, but the 43rd man to hold the office. He defeated Republican nominee John McCain in the general election, and was inaugurated as president on January 20, 2009. Nine months later, Obama was named the 2009 Nobel Peace Prize laureate. He was re-elected president in November 2012, defeating Republican nominee Mitt Romney. He is the first Democrat since Franklin D. Roosevelt to win two presidential elections with a majority of the popular vote, who would have thought that an African American would be made President of the United States of America. You may read more about President Obama at: http://en.wikipedia.org/wiki/Barack_Obama

- **Susan Boyle**—a committed Christian, with the voice of an angel and practically an undiscovered talent appeared on Britain's Got Talent 2009 on 11th April 2009. She was propelled onto the world's stage, where she was sought after by the A-listers and crème de la crème of society. Prime Ministers, Presidents and Ambassadors of countries courted her. Her first album *I Dreamed a Dream* was released on 23rd November 2009 and debuted as the number one best-selling CD on charts around the globe.

- Her success continued with her second album, The Gift (2010), and was followed by her third album, Someone to Watch Over Me, released on 31 October 2011. On 12 May 2012, Susan returned to Britain's Got Talent to perform as a guest in the final singing "You'll See". The following day, she performed at Windsor Castle for the Queen's Diamond Jubilee Pageant singing "Mull of Kintyre" Boyle's net worth was estimated at £22 million in April 2012. You may read more about her Susan Boyle at: http://en.wikipedia.org/wiki/Susan_Boyle

- **Michael Jackson**—born on 29th August 1958. He was an American musician, dancer, and entertainer. He was often referred to as the King of Pop; he was the most commercially successful and one of the most influential entertainers of all time. His unique contributions to music, dance, and fashion made him a prominent figure in popular culture for over four decades. His 1982 album *Thriller* remains the best-selling album of all time, with *Off the Wall* (1979), *Bad* (1987), *Dangerous* (1991), and HIStory (1995) being among the world's best selling albums. He is widely credited with having transformed the music video from a promotional tool into an art making him the first African American artist to amass a strong crossover following on MTV. His distinctive musical sound, vocal style and choreography have inspired numerous artists and he is credited with breaking down cultural, racial, and generational barriers.

  Michael Jackson's death triggered a global outpouring of grief, and as many as one billion people around the world reportedly watched his public memorial service on live television. In March 2010, Sony Music Entertainment and Jackson's estate signed the largest music contract ever, with a $250 million deal to retain distribution rights to his recordings until 2017, and to release seven posthumous albums over the decade following his death. You may read more about Michael Jackson at: http://en.wikipedia.org/wiki/Michael_Jackson

The United Kingdom hosted the London 2012 Olympic Games which saw a hosts of participants achieve tremendous feats. These participants showed sheer determination, skill and drive. Purpose and destinies were fulfilled in front of the whole world. Some of these participants were:-

- **Eleanor Simmonds** –At aged 13 years she won two gold medals when she swam at the 2008 Beijing Paralympics and is now crowned Britain's youngest individual medallist. She was born with dwarfism syndrome, which made the likelihood of her becoming a great swimmer impossible. However despite her disability, she reached for the top. She said after her victory ""I can't believe that I'm a champion. I imagined this race in a dream". Determination and courage saw her fulfil her dream. In 2008 she won the BBC Young Sports Personality of the Year award. In 2009, at aged 14 years she was appointed a Member of the Order of the British Empire (MBE). She is the youngest person to ever receive this award.

  In 2012 she was again selected for the Great Britain squad, this time swimming at home games in London. She won two gold medals in London, including setting a World Record in the 400m freestyle. You may read more about Eleanor Simmonds at: http://en.wikipedia.org/wiki/Eleanor_Simmonds

- **Usain Bolt**—born on 21st August 1986 in Jamaica. He put Jamaica on the world map as a serious contender on the field of sports by taking the world by storm during the 2008 Olympics. He now holds the Olympic and world records for the 100 meters race at 9.69 seconds and the 200 meters race at 19.30 seconds. He also holds the 4 x 400 meters relay at 37.10 seconds with his team mates. He is the first man to win all three sprinting events at a single Olympic event and the first man in history to set world records in all three events at a single Olympic event. In 2009, he became the first man to hold the 100 and 200 meters world and

> Olympic titles at the same time. Because of his remarkable success on the field, he has now been given the nickname of "'Lightning' Bolt". As a result of his successes in athletics, he was named the Laureus World Sportsman of the Year for 2009 and 2010.
>
> He is the reigning Olympic champion, the first man to win six Olympic gold medals in sprinting, and a five-time World champion. He was the first to achieve a "double double" by winning 100 m and 200 m titles at consecutive Olympics (2008 and 2012), and topped this through the first "double triple" (including 4x100m relays). He has been called the world's most marketable athlete and the greatest athlete ever. You may read more about Usain Bolt at: http://en.wikipedia.org/wiki/Usain_Bolt

The world will hear from you like the above-mentioned persons because God has bestowed upon you His blessings far beyond your imagination or your expectation. God has birth inside of you endless possibilities. You can do anything you set you mind at. You must reach forth to the Heavens and take hold of your possessions.

Despite the odds, all these persons succeeded. You too will succeed. When God says He will do it, rest assured that He will do what He says He will do. God is taking you somewhere; it is your duty to get prepared and ready for the journey ahead.

Psalm 30:7 states that by God's favour He has established us as a strong mountain. God has made us a little lower than Himself, greater than angels. He has given us dominion over the works of His hands and has put all things under our feet (*Psalm 8*). Therefore go out into the world and become an overcomer and a winner. Remember always that your God is a God of endless and outstanding possibilities; therefore nothing is impossible for you to achieve in His Name.

In my own personal life, God has done great things for me of which I am thankful for. He has given my life meaning. I had spent most of my childhood blocking out my life's experiences that I couldn't reach forth to take hold of God's blessings. I had blocked out my past hurts and not appreciated the many blessings God had bestowed upon me, like being in good health, succeeding in my dreams of becoming a lawyer and serving in His vineyard. I am now able to appreciate God's Saving Grace. When I needed someone to hold my hands during those trying times, God was there, when I needed a shoulder to lean on, He was there and when I needed someone to understand my pain, He was there, these are all blessings from God and I am thankful to Him for these.

My story has not ended yet, this is not the final chapter of my life as I am still a work in progress. There is still so much more for me to achieve and do. I am still pressing on towards the finish line that God has set for me. **I know with Christ in my life I will reach the mark and fulfil my purpose.**

God is in Control of Your Life

But [even] the very hairs of your head are all numbered. Do not be struck with fear or seized with alarm; you are of greater worth than many [flocks] of sparrows' Luke 12:7 (AMP).

Know for sure that God is in control of your life for you are of more worth to Him than many flocks of Sparrow. If you have ever wondered whether this is true, wonder no further as God knows when a strand of hair falls from your head. God is the Guiding Force that controls the universe; He is in control of your life, the church and government. He wraps things up by having satan under His feet.

God sees everything and knows everything. He knows when you have been tried, tempted and tested. He will preserve your life for the best, as He knows how your future will turn out.

Knowing that God is in control of your life should keep your mind at peace. He will give you the wisdom to control your environment and use the resources available on this earth for your own advantage. God's blessings will never pass you by.

The longer I live, the more convincing proofs I see of this truth, that God governs in the affairs of man; and if a sparrow cannot fall to the ground without His notice, is it probable that an empire can rise without His aid?
-Benjamin Franklin

Providence will Speak Out for You

God will not abandon you to fate; your plans and intents may be in your heart but it is God who sanctions them. The Lord directs the steps of the righteous and He exercises Lordship over their spirit. God is never absent from your life and He will direct the outcome of your life — if you allow Him to do so. He will speak out for you when occasion demands it. God works everything together for your good; He will cause you to get noticed and elevated despite the opposition of others.

Providence will prevent others from stealing your blessing and limelight by giving you inner courage to stand up and be heard. Don't allow people to mould you into what they believe you should become, take strength in the knowledge that God is in charge of your life and things will eventually turn out the way He has "willed" it.

Trust the past to God's mercy, the present to God's love, and the future to God's Providence.—St. Augustine

Balance Your Life

Have a reality check about where you are and what you want to achieve in life. Know that with God on your side, you can achieve anything.

Stop rushing through life trying to achieve everything all at once, stop for a moment and put things into perspective. In order for you to succeed in life you need to make rational decisions, when you fail to balance your life, you take the wrong actions and fail to achieve anything significant.

God is the corner stone of your life, when you make Him your Rock, you will never be disappointed.

The expectation of the righteous will never fail. You must have a Godly confidence that what He has promised will come to pass. Balance your expectation of people, family and friends, don't expect from them that which they cannot reasonably give or deliver as God is the only One who can meet your life's expectations. I am not saying don't trust people or expect much from them but that there is only a limit a human being can do for you. Your dependence and reliance must be in God alone.

Your life is what you choose to make it, have a balanced view of life and things will work out well for you.

Abstain from every form of evil. Now may the God of peace Himself sanctify you completely; and may your whole spirit, soul, and body be preserved blameless at the coming of our Lord Jesus Christ. He who calls you is faithful, who also will do it. (1 Thessalonians 5:22-24).

Patience is a Virtue

We all so quickly say "patience is a virtue" but do we really understand its meaning? Can you change anything by being impatient with God? No matter how much we fret, we cannot turn God's hands around. God's promises will come to pass no matter what we do; your patience will go a long way.

Your ability to wait for your desired result without grumbling or complaining is a virtue. Your ability to wait calmly when faced with challenges is to be commended.

Patience will save you from failing, falling and faltering. Faith, hope and patience will save you from many a shame.

You will keep him in perfect peace; Whose mind is stayed on You, Because he trusts in You. Trust in the LORD forever, For in JEHOVAH, the LORD, is everlasting strength. (Isaiah 26:3-4)

Conclusion

You were created to be blessed and to be a blessing to your generation, therefore rise up and fulfil your God given mandate.

Delight yourself in God and desire Him above everything else and He will fulfil all the desires of your heart just as He has promised. Exercise the divine mandate given to you at creation by taking authority over every situation and circumstance. Utilise all the resources on this earth for your benefit and become a blessing to your generation. Seize the moment and take hold of your blessings, don't procrastinate any longer.

Don't try to assist God or force His hand as you wait for your miracle. There is nothing too hard for the Lord to do; what He has promised, He will surely bring to pass.

May God's peace continue to garrison your heart, mind and soul; may His peace continually flow through you like a river. Amen.

God's blessings will come to you at the appointed time (Habakkuk 2:3).

Thanks so much for reading this book. I hope you enjoyed it and have now opened up your heart, mind and soul to receive all that God has in store for you.

I pray that God's blessings, Grace and Spirit will be bestowed upon you

If you have found this book helpful, kindly provide your reviews on the website you purchased a copy of this book from or the various publishing platforms such as Amazon, CreateSpace and Lulu.

Other Books by Author

Become All That God Has Created You To Be

The Beginners' Guide to Wealth Creation

A Simple Guide to UK Immigration

The Beginners' Guide to Writing, Self-Publishing and Marketing a Book

Purpose2Destiny TK Limited

P O BOX 3162

Romford

RM3 9WR
United Kingdom

www.ingramcontent.com/pod-product-compliance
Lightning Source LLC
LaVergne TN
LVHW010105110826
845155LV00028B/497

9781909787087